THE
BIKE
BOOK

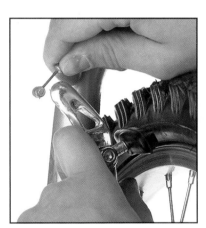  

Meredith® Press

Des Moines, Iowa

Contents

Written and edited by: Fred Milson
Studio photography: Steve Behr
Tim Ridley
Polly Wreford
Illustrations: Ian Bott
Art director: Norma Martin
Designer: Peter Charles
Production manager: Kevin Perrett
Managing editor: Miranda Spicer
Project manager: Kevin Hudson

Fred Milson has asserted his right to be
identified as the author of this work.

American edition published 1997

© Haynes Publishing 1995

Published by:
Meredith Corporation
1716 Locust Street
Des Moines, IA 50309-3023

ISBN: 0-696-20690-0

Printed in Italy by G. Canale & C.

CHAPTER 5
Chain, Pedals & Cranks

CHAPTER 6
Braking Systems

CHAPTER 7
Wheels & Tires

CHAPTER 8
Bars & Saddles

CHAPTER 9
Frame & Forks

CHAPTER 10
Bike Extras

# Welcome to

Here is a book designed and written for every kind of cyclist. Featuring mountain bikes, commuter bikes, road bikes, hybrids, and children's bikes, it gives details of how to tackle every job that you can reasonably expect to do without having to make a massive investment in special tools.

Simply riding a bike can give you enormous pleasure and satisfaction, but add to this the ability to do your own repairs and you'll feel more skilled and self-reliant. You'll need the expert guidance of this book to start with but after a while it'll all become second nature.

The first things you'll need to grasp are the names of the parts of a bicycle, as well as the different styles of bike on the road. That is how the book starts. It then goes on to tell you how to set up a good riding position for both children and adults. In the second chapter, the book explains how to build up a small tool kit and teaches you how to use it without damaging the components you're working on, giving a few tricks of the trade for solving common problems. The third chapter details five routines for looking after your bike; none should take more than 10 minutes once you've built up a bit of skill. In fact, chapter 3 contains crucial information on how to clean your bike, how to keep it lubricated, how to keep the tires properly maintained, and how to be aware of developing problems so that they can be addressed before becoming serious. Paying attention to this chapter should mean a bike that rides smoothly, freely, silently and comfortably.

The rest of the book is devoted to maintenance and repair. Each chapter covers a separate component system of the bike and starts by telling you how to check for wear, how to replace the parts that are most likely to need replacing and how to upgrade any parts of your bike that don't really suit the sort of riding that you do. All the stages of the job are shown in pictures but the text gives you vital background knowledge. A comprehensive glossary titled "What Does That Mean?" leads you through bike jargon and explains how each part fits into the workings of the whole bike. Finally, there is a troubleshooting guide to help diagnose problems with your bicycle.

The Bike Book

CHAPTER 1

KNOW YOUR BIKE

This book has been written using just a few technical words and close to zero cycling jargon. But you will find it an easier read if you pick up a few essential words right at the start.

Name that part

OTHER STYLES OF SADDLES

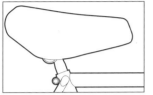

WOMEN'S SADDLE
Specially designed saddle, can be fitted to almost any bike.

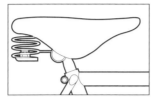

MATTRESS SADDLE
For utility bikes only.

SADDLE

SEAT POST

CABLE STOP

TOP TUBE

SEAT TUBE

WHEEL NUTS

REAR BRAKE

FRONT DERAILLEU

SPROCKET CLUSTER
AND FREEWHEEL

DOWN TUBE

ALTERNATIVE GEARING SYSTEMS

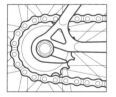

SINGLE SPEED FREEWHEEL
Mainly used on kids' bikes.

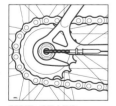

HUB GEARS
As used on most utility bikes and some cruisers.

CHAINRI

CRANKS

BOTTOM
BRACKET

PEDAL

GEAR CABLE

CHAIN

REAR DERAILLEUR

CHAIN STAYS ·

ALTERNATIVE HANDLEBARS

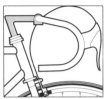

DROP HANDLE-BARS
For road racing and touring bikes.

FLATS
For hybrids and utilities.

RAISED BARS
Used on utilities only.

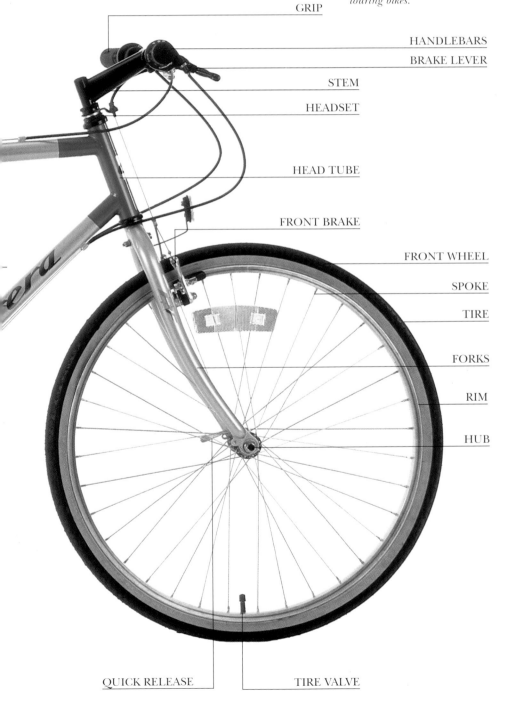

GRIP

HANDLEBARS

BRAKE LEVER

STEM

HEADSET

HEAD TUBE

FRONT BRAKE

FRONT WHEEL

SPOKE

TIRE

FORKS

RIM

HUB

QUICK RELEASE

TIRE VALVE

VARIOUS TYPES OF TIRE

KNOBBY TIRES
For off-road mountain bikes.

MOUNTAIN BIKE SLICKS
For use on the road.

700 C or 27 INCH
Tires for road bikes and hybrids.

Adults' bikes

In the last ten years, mountain bikes have outsold every other type. But you should still ask yourself whether another style wouldn't suit you better and also think about bringing an old bike back into use with a little tender loving care.

In the United States about three-quarters of the new bikes sold in the '90s have been mountain bikes (MTB's). But road bikes still sell and, like the top mountain bikes, now use technologies and materials developed in the aerospace industry. However, the latest category to emerge is the hybrid bike, which has a small frame, 27-inch wheels and MTB brakes, gears and frame fittings. They combine the speed of a road bike with the capability of an MTB.

But if there is one thing this book shows, it's that any bike of any age can be put back on the road with a little bit of effort and some investment.

MOUNTAIN BIKES
The key to mountain bike popularity is versatility. The small frames and 26-inch wheels with well-cushioned tires originated in California among riders who enjoyed plummeting down mountain sides. By coincidence, the same features suit city riders who need to bump up and down curbs and ride through potholes. And even though many MTB riders insist on dressing the part, civilian clothes are entirely suitable.

ROAD BIKE

Like mountain bikes, road bikes range from budget-priced everyday bikes to $4,000 true racers. On pavement, road bikes are faster than MTBs but not so comfortable because much of their advantage comes from ultra thin, 27-inch wheels. Road bikes take minor city potholes in stride, but you can't jump curbs with them.

WOMEN'S BIKE

An open frame gives the option of riding in a skirt if desired. Sporty drop handlebar models are still used in large numbers but a mountain bike with a sloping top tube is another possible option.

UTILITY BIKE

Popular for city use over short distances, the upright riding position means you can wear fairly formal clothes and still cycle to work. Not fast enough or fun enough for leisure riding.

HYBRID BIKE

The basis of a hybrid is the modified MTB frame, often with a sloping top tube. Not only does this keep the frame light and agile at low speeds, it also gives a lot more clearance over the top tube when you wait at traffic lights or jump curbs. Look for brazed-on carrier fittings and robust but light wheels and tires when you're buying. Or consider 'hybridizing' an MTB or a cast-off road bike.

Adults' bike setup

A good riding position doesn't just make you comfortable, it helps you to expand the chest and breathe deeply. And you will be less likely to get aches and pains the day after.

When you acquire a bike, set the riding position using the advice on the opposite page. Then ride around for a few days to get used to it. The new bike may be strange at first but if the riding position is roughly right, you will feel that your weight is being shared fairly evenly between the saddle and the handlebars. In addition, you shouldn't have to stretch to find a suitable hand position. Experiment until you're sure you've got things right but don't move far from the standard position without expert advice.

If you're not comfortable on the saddle, check that it's horizontal and, if it is, try moving it half an inch forward. Some riders feel better with the saddle nose pointed up just one degree or so but don't go any farther than that. Install a different saddle if you really can't get comfortable.

Ideally, handlebars on a road bike should be the same width as your shoulders and your back should be around forty five degrees to the ground when your hands are in their usual position. If you feel squashed up when riding, it may be worth lowering the handlebars or changing to a stem with a longer extension.

Most people buy frames that are too large, often because retailers prefer to stock the bigger sizes, knowing they can drop the saddle for shorter riders if necessary. Some experts suggest you should have a couple of inches clearance over the top tube on a road racing bike while touring frames should be slightly larger, allowing an inch clearance. But whatever type of bike you're after, don't let yourself be talked into the wrong size as the proportions of the frame will be all wrong.

UTILITY BIKES
Frames on utility bikes are normally laid well back, so most weight falls on the saddle. There is no way of avoiding this completely but you could try lowering the handlebars or substituting straight ones if you're really uncomfortable. Toe clips aren't usually put on utilities but try to keep the ball of your foot over the pedal axle to improve pedalling efficiency.

Frame size

1 Measure from the center of the bottom bracket axle to the point where the center of the top tube cuts across the seat lug to get the frame size. Some makers quote this in inches, others in centimeters but most use this center-to-center method.

2 Frames for road racers, touring bikes and men's utility bikes are all roughly the same height from floor to top tube. You should aim for an inch and a half or so of clearance between the top tube and your crotch, when your feet are planted flat on the floor.

3 Mountain bike frames have a different shape, partly to ensure you have at least three inches clearance over a horizontal top tube. But many recent MTBs have a sloping top tube, and with this shape of frame, top tube clearance should be five or six inches.

Saddle position

1 Always set the saddle height first to give you a starting point in the adjustment process. Wear the shoes you will usually ride in and position the saddle so that your leg is very slightly bent when the pedal is at the lowest point.

2 Make a plumb line with a piece of string and a small weight and turn the cranks so they're horizontal. Adjust the saddle position until a plumb line hanging from the back of your knee cap lines up with the ball of your foot.

Kids' bikes

When kids ride a bike, they gain so many things: self-confidence, the beginnings of mechanical skills, road sense . . . even adventure. Provided they get good training in road skills right from the start, it's a very positive experience.

Parents usually enter the shop determined to buy a bike that is far too large. Don't. The recipient will find it much more difficult to ride. The BMX style is strong and easy to ride, so it's ideal for youngsters ages six and older. But make sure the brakes don't disappear as there is a street fashion for having no brakes at all.

Eleven-year-olds and upwards can safely ride a mountain bike with 26-inch wheels. But, if the gears keep getting out of whack, set the adjusting screws so the rear derailleur won't change out of middle gear until kids are old enough to use them sensibly.

MOUNTAIN BIKE
From eleven onwards, an adult-style mountain bike is fine. If you look for one with a 14- or 15-inch frame and a sloping top tube, there will be plenty of standover clearance and it will allow for a considerable amount of growth. Don't forget you can install a longer seat post in the years to come but toe clips should be added only for kids twelve or older. If you plan to keep the bike for some time, it might be worth going for a bike one or two steps up from budget level because the higher-quality components will need less maintenance and they will also be easier to work on.

BMX BIKES
Maybe the most suitable style of bike for adventurous kids, BMXs are strictly minimum maintenance. The frames are strong, there are no gears to jam or get bent and they have plenty of street appeal—probably more than a mountain bike. And although some of the BMX tricks look frightening, the frames are so small that kids don't have far to fall.

TRAINING-WHEEL BIKE
OK for giving the very youngest children a taste for cycling but they can become a substitute for learning to ride properly.

MOUNTAIN BIKE WITH 20-INCH WHEELS
These are scaled down mountain bikes with small wheels, enabling kids ages seven or eight and up to ride them. But they have the multiple gearing system of an adult MTB, which will probably need a lot of maintenance.

GIRL'S BIKE
Now that the sloping top tube frame is used on most kids' bikes, there is really no point in buying a girl's bike as the top tube is only a few inches lower anyway.

Kids' bike setup

Don't leave your child's riding position to chance or the other kids. Set it up carefully for safety and easy control.

Until your children have mastered adult level bike control and road awareness, insist on setting their riding position and check it occasionally as they grow. The main thing is to keep the saddle low enough to allow them to plant both feet flat on the ground with the legs straight. This should give plenty of standover clearance above the top tube but check that there's at least two inches on a conventional bike or at least three on a sloping top tube frame. Don't forget to check the reach as well. If a child has to lean forward to reach the handlebars, maybe you should install a stem with a shorter extension. Whatever the style of bike, children should sit more upright than adults to encourage

them to look ahead down the road. As they get older, you can raise the saddle a bit more but err on the side of safety.

Parents report that the easiest way to teach kids how to ride is to set the saddle height with the child's feet on the floor, bike upright and legs slightly bent. Then remove the pedals as explained on page 78 and let the kid loose. They'll naturally start to scoot the bike along with their feet, learning how to steer and use the brakes as they go. Once they've gained some confidence, the saddle can be raised little by little until they're starting to lift both feet off the ground. At that point, introduce straight line and slalom exercises and once they can steer accurately, on with the pedals and away!

FEET FLAT ON THE GROUND
Until a child has nearly perfect bike control, keep the saddle low so that she can get her feet down quickly if necessary. This'll help to prevent scraped knees and bike damage as well. It'll also allow more than enough clearance over the top tube. This bike has 20-inch wheels with reflectors on the spokes to draw the motorist's attention both day and night. To be truly equipped for after-dark, this bike should also have headlights and taillights.

WRONG POSITION
Not only is the rider perched on the saddle and forced to extend his legs fully to reach the pedals, he's also stretching to reach the handlebars. This is forcing him to adopt a crouching position, which is uncomfortable and discourages the rider from looking far enough ahead.

STAY IN YOUR PLACE
When you're out with the children, insist they ride in front of you so that you can see everything that's happening. But don't ride too close or you'll have to keep on braking and there's also the danger of a crash if somebody in front stops unexpectedly.

SLOPING TOP TUBE
The sloping top tube design also works well for younger children, giving plenty of standover height.

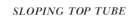

SPECIAL PARTS
Most kids' bikes are small versions of an adult's bike. But some have special headsets and cranksets that work in a very different way. The headsets are similar to the Aheadset featured on page 148, while the crankset and bottom bracket are covered on page 92.

TINY BIKES FOR TINIES
An enclosed space or garden is best for very young riders, where they can pick up self confidence in complete safety. Set up a slalom course and figure-eight steering tests for fun and to exercise control skills.

Personal safety

Whether or not your state has a helmet law, it's smarter not to venture on a road or trail without a helmet.

Don't rush in and buy a helmet in the first shop you come to. Find one that has a good selection of helmets from a wide variety of different makers and employs experienced staff. Then ask them to advise you about fit and suitability for your kind of cycling.

Try on plenty of types of helmet and don't give up until you find one with a firm fit, even if you feel it is just sitting on the top of your head. If you are able to move it backwards and forwards with the chin strap fastened, it's too big. Not only will it be uncomfortable, it will also give you less protection and may even slip off when it's put to the test.

Apart from fit, the other factor governing comfort is ventilation. Make sure there are plenty of air channels running from front to back because although a helmet may not feel hot in the shop, it certainly will after ten miles' hard pedalling.

Above all, go for a good standard of manufacture and testing. Look for an ANSI, ASTM, or a Snell sticker inside to be sure the helmet meets current safety requirements.

CRASHED HAT
The shock absorbing material in a helmet compresses during a crash and doesn't regenerate, so you have to get a new one any time it takes a heavy blow, even if you're off your bike and carrying the helmet. Why not go for one of the more expensive makes offering free replacement?

1 Make sure you buy a well-fitting helmet. If it's right, it will sit high enough above your brow to allow unobstructed vision when you're looking upwards or sideways. And when you wiggle your ears, the helmet will move with your scalp.

2 Check from the side that it sits level and that the straps fit well. If they gape or the helmet keeps on riding up and back, try a different make. Don't rely on sizing pads to solve basic problems of size or shape, use for final adjustments only.

The child's helmet above has solar system graphics, air channels and extra sizing pads to allow for growth. Below is a more conventional, adult helmet with aerodynamic refinements.

WRONG HEADED
It's hard to tell front from back of most helmets. Hardly surprising, as the shape is more about styling than anything else, unless you go for one of the uncompromisingly aerodynamic styles. But the straps will give it away because they must fit comfortably on either side of the ears, anchoring the helmet comfortably but firmly. Be careful not to twist the straps either.

3 A kid's helmet must fit like an adult's would, but look for one that can take extra sizing pads to allow for growth. When the strap is comfortable, the helmet should feel firm on the head and you shouldn't be able to move it independently.

CHAPTER 2

TOOLS & TECHNIQUES

Take a look at the tools you've already got in the house and the garage – you will probably have to buy just a few extra ones before starting work on your bike. Then have a look at some ideas about how to use them.

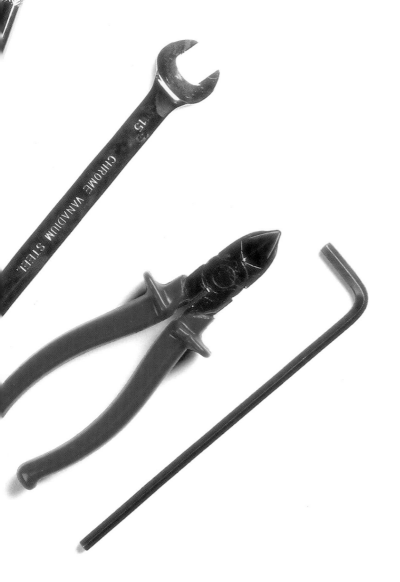

Basic tool kit

If you're looking after your bike properly, you will probably spend around half of your maintenance time cleaning and oiling the chain and the gear mechanisms.

Provided you've got most of the tools shown on this page, the main things you will need to buy before starting work are bike-friendly lubricants. Aerosol spray lube is used for most jobs and the best types leave a solid lubricant behind when they evaporate. But, for chains, many cyclists recommend backing up the solid lubricant with a heavier oil. Even if it gets washed off in a downpour, the heavy oil will repel water most of the time. These lubricants also work well on cables. You won't need grease until you're ready to strip down the bearings. Use a waterproof grade specially formulated for bikes – ordinary greases thicken up with age and break down if water penetrates the bearings.

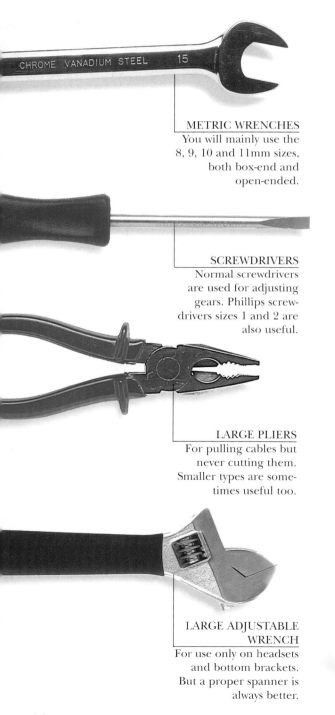

METRIC WRENCHES
You will mainly use the 8, 9, 10 and 11mm sizes, both box-end and open-ended.

SCREWDRIVERS
Normal screwdrivers are used for adjusting gears. Phillips screwdrivers sizes 1 and 2 are also useful.

LARGE PLIERS
For pulling cables but never cutting them. Smaller types are sometimes useful too.

LARGE ADJUSTABLE WRENCH
For use only on headsets and bottom brackets. But a proper spanner is always better.

HEAVY OIL

GREASE SOLVENT

WATERPROOF GREASE

CLEANING AND ANTI-SEIZE

HAND CLEANER

ANTI-SEIZE COMPOUND

OILS AND GREASES

SPRAY LUBE

SPRAY LUBE

TOOTHBRUSH
You will find it easier and quicker degreasing components with a toothbrush than anything else.

UTILITY KNIFE
For cutting handlebar tape, electrical insulation and zip ties.

GREASE INJECTOR PACK

ALLEN KEYS
The standard type is shown here but the long work-shop type is much more useful on bikes. You will need sizes up to 8 or 10 mm.

GRAPHITED GREASE
This is the same as the anti-seize compound and can be used inter-changeably.

BALLPEEN HAMMER
A 16- or 20-ounce hammer is excellent for sharp, accurate blows. This type of hammer is much less likely to slip than others.

Working techniques

Getting hold of the tools is one thing, but now you've got to start using them without damaging the things you are working on.

Nuts and bolts have a six-sided shape which is usually spoken of as a hexagon. Damage the hexagon with a badly fitting wrench and it will be a nuisance until the day you replace it. To avoid this, use a tightly fitting box-end wrench whenever you can. If you have to use an open-ended wrench and it feels loose on the hexagon, try to find one with a better fit. If you can't, try wedging a small coin or a washer in the jaws of the wrench to take up the slack.

The length of each wrench is related to the amount of force needed to tighten each size of nut, so don't use a lot of force. You should be able to tighten up anything sufficiently using the pull of three fingers. If the amount of effort required to tighten a nut or bolt suddenly increases, stop immediately as something is about to break. You can apply a bit of extra force if something keeps on coming loose but it's better to put on a self-locking nut or use Loctite.

Allen-head bolts look great on bikes because they are so neat. But, unlike nuts or bolts, which you can nearly always remove one way or another, damaged Allen-head bolts are almost impossible to remove. So check that the socket is clean and make sure the Allen key is an exact fit. Don't use silver-painted Allen keys as they are made of soft metal and usually fit very badly. If you've got a handful of mixed Allen keys, check the size which is engraved on the side of good-quality Allen keys and use the metric ones only on your bike. If you want the ultimate in workshop Allen keys, go for the ones with T-handles.

Phillips screws also look very neat but are even more liable to damage. The way to guard against this is to use Phillips screwdrivers with hardened tips only. Even this type wears, so check that all four ribs have straight, undamaged sides and a sharp tip.

1 Whenever possible, use a box-end wrench or socket wrench in preference to any other type. They grip a nut or bolt on all six corners, so if you're careful, there is little chance of slipping and damaging the hexagon.

2 Compared to a box-end wrench, an open-ended wrench is more likely to slip because it grips only two corners. When you've no choice but to use one, prevent it from slipping by steadying your hand against another component.

5 Allen-head bolts tend to fill with mud. So clean any dirt out and check that the Allen key goes all the way to the base of the socket, before applying pressure. Otherwise the Allen key may slip in the socket and damage it.

6 When an Allen-head bolt is buried deep in a component, you will only be able to reach it with the long leg of the Allen key. To increase the leverage, if necessary, slip a close-fitting length of tubing over the shorter end.

3 Once you've got a set of open-ended wrenches, you will find they also come in useful for holding bolts while you loosen the nut. You will need to do this when a bolt turns before the nut comes undone and on most cable carriers.

4 Socket sets aren't usually regarded as bike tools but they are ideal for jobs where the nut is buried. On some pedals, for example, you can only reach the cone locknut with a socket and extension. They are also good on crank bolts.

8 When metal gets damaged, it's often possible to bend it back again, gripping it in a vice or using a couple of adjustable wrenches. But this rearranges all the molecules in the metal and so tends to harden it. This work-hardening effect doesn't take place immediately, so try to repair the damage in one go, not a series of separate small adjustments.

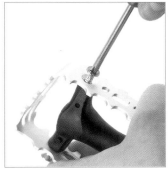

7 Phillips screws crop up on derailleurs and pedals. Check that the screwdriver isn't worn and position it in a straight line with the screw before you apply pressure, or it might slip and make it difficult to remove the screw at all.

Preventing future problems

When you tighten up something, remember that some day you will want to unbolt it again. If you do it right, that shouldn't be a problem.

If you've ever worked on a secondhand bike or an old house, you've probably come across problems caused by bad workmanship or by ignoring well-known principles. Assuming you're going to keep your bike for a while, you need to know and should always apply the basics of Good Workshop Practice, otherwise you will have to put up with the consequences as they emerge.

When assembling components, bolt them up firmly but not so tight that you damage the threads. Be particularly careful with alloy parts because they usually have a deep coarse thread and it's quite easy to cross-thread them. Try to hold things with your fingertips when you start to screw them into place and back off immediately if the amount of force needed to turn something suddenly increases.

Use self-locking nuts to stop things from vibrating and coming undone. Theoretically you should use a new one each time but on bikes, the forces involved are not great and so you can use them indefinitely. If you can't use a self-locking nut on something but need to make sure it stays tight, use Loctite. This is a chemical that you apply to a clean thread and which is only activated when something is tightened. Once set, the nut or bolt shouldn't come undone until you use a wrench on it.

Good tools make any job easy and keep a bike looking good because they don't damage the six-sided or hexagonal heads on nuts and bolts. Worn or damaged tools make a job harder and in some cases make it difficult to complete a job, even with good tools. This also applies to using adjustable wrenches and pliers of every sort instead of proper, well-fitting wrenches and spanners.

Be especially careful when putting two metals in contact with each other. If there is any water around, it will create an electrical circuit and the non-steel component can corrode pretty quickly, making it very difficult to separate them. If you've no anti-seize compound, oil or grease is better than nothing. Car accessory shops are more likely to stock anti-seize than bike shops.

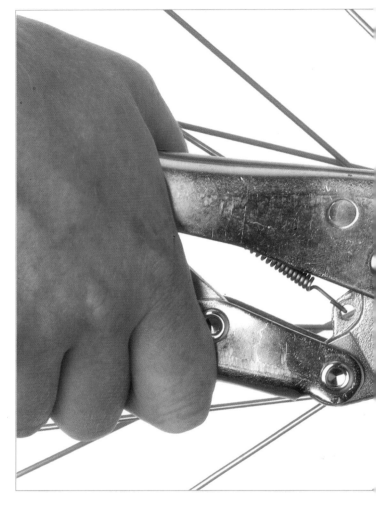

1 Self-locking nuts grip the thread of the bolt with a nylon insert and so they won't vibrate loose. Use them when you install toe clips, lighting equipment, mudguards and luggage carriers. On bikes it is OK to re-use them.

2 Anti-seize compound must be used when putting two different metals in close contact with each other. This applies whether you are screwing a steel pedal axle into an alloy crank or putting an alloy seat post into a steel frame.

3 Don't use worn wrenches because they will damage the nuts and bolts you use them on. The first thing that goes is usually the chrome inside the jaws but thin wrenches can spring open if they are misused. This often happens to cone wrenches.

4 Special tools like freewheel removers often get worn or damaged because of the force you apply when using them. So before you start, check them carefully and make sure you've got exactly the right one for the job. The wrong tool can cause hefty damage.

5 Corrosion can easily get a hold inside brake and gear cables, causing problems like poor gear changing and high lever effort. The best way to prevent this is to fire spray lube or drip light mineral oil down every outer cable housing before intalling them.

6 Self-locking pliers have no place at all in a bike workshop. Nor do water pump pliers or slip joint pliers. They all tend to damage not only the nut or bolt you want to undo but also any soft alloy surfaces or paintwork in the vicinity.

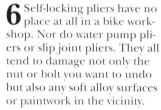

7 When stripping components like chain wheels and derailleurs, lay the small parts, particularly the washers and spacers, out in order as you take them off. Keep them facing the same way that they were installed.

8 The only time you should use a hammer is when altering the height of the handlebars. One sharp blow should normally do it but if you have to give something else a tap, cushion the blow with a cloth or a piece of wood.

LONG TERM STORAGE

When a bike is out of use, the tires go down and, once that has happened, they deteriorate fast. If you think you're not going to use your bike for a month, repair any punctures, including slow leaks, and pump the tires up harder than normal. If you're not going to use it for months, oil the chain, gears, pedals and hubs with heavy oil. And hang it up out of the sun or the ultraviolet rays will speed up the deterioration of any rubber and plastic components.

When you come back after a few years, all the grease will have combined with oxygen and lost its lubricating qualities. It's best to strip, clean and regrease all the bearings before you use the bike again.

Working on cables

There are four cables on most bikes and if they are put on badly, you will have endless trouble. But properly installed cables help ensure that your bike runs smoothly and reliably.

As explained later in Chapter 4, the main thing when installing gear cables is that indexed gears must be installed with both inner cable and outer cable housing manufactured to suit indexed gears. So far as the inners are concerned, they are usually pre-stretched to minimize the need for adjustment and specially treated to reduce friction. The housings are made from separate wires running along the cable, not from spiral-wound flat wire like standard cable housing. This special construction reduces the springiness of the housing, as does installing metal ferrules. Derailleurs are usually supplied with ready-made sealed cable housings and if you can get hold of them, always use this type.

Shimano housing is always marked with the name. It's probably easier to find than other makes and will work fine with other indexing systems. When cutting it, use the special Shimano tool which is designed to cope with this housing construction. This tool also has a pair of jaws for shaping the cut ends of the housing. It will also cut standard cable housing without any problems.

All brakes will work perfectly well with any brake cable but you have to be careful to get the correct nipple to fit in the brake lever. Dia Compe levers in particular use an extra large nipple.

Inspecting cables

1 The most likely place for a cable to fray is below the anchor bolt. This doesn't usually affect the strength of the cable but you won't be able to tighten it up very easily. Install a new cable when convenient because the fraying will eventually spread and weaken the old one.

2 Fraying usually starts at the end of the cable or near the cable hanger. Sometimes you can get away with cutting off each wire that has come unwound but eventually a cut end will lift inside the housing and stop the cable from moving smoothly. Install a new one immediately.

Cutting standard cable housings

1 To cut standard cable housing, squeeze the cutter lightly so the jaws slide between the coils of wire first. Then squeeze harder to cut.

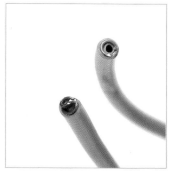

2 If the wire cutter leaves a jagged end as on the bottom housing, clean it up with the cutters or a grinder so it's like the top one before fitting.

3 When replacing outer cable housing, use the old one as a pattern so you get the length right. Or cut slightly too long and measure against the bike.

4 Ideally, housings should be installed with a metal ferrule at each end. They protect the plastic outer covering and ensure the housings seat squarely in the cable stops.

5 Don't try to fit a new inner cable into a damaged housing as it will probably start to fray. If this happens, pull the inner cable back and try re-cutting the damaged end.

Finishing touches

1 Once you've checked that the derailleur or the brake is working properly, cut off any spare cable with your cutters and pinch a cable endcap on the end using pliers.

2 The usual way to tension a cable is to pull it with pliers but it's not always easy to do so. It's easier to use a fourth-hand tool which cuts out the need for extra hands.

TOOLS FOR WORKING ON CABLES

WIRE CUTTERS
◆ **You need a good pair of wire cutters before you start replacing cables. Ordinary pliers often include wire cutters but they tend to squash the cable, not cut it. Don't buy cheap wire cutters as they often do the same thing.**

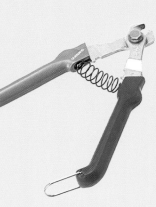

SHIMANO CABLE TOOL
◆ **Shimano wire cutters are the only tool suitable for cutting Shimano cable housing.**

FOURTH-HAND TOOL
◆ **These are better than a third-hand tool because you can use them on gears as well as brakes.**

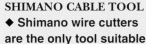

Problem solving

Maybe you've inherited problems with an old bike, maybe you've fouled up something yourself. Luckily most bike problems can be fixed with a bit of cunning.

Stick to the instructions and advice in this book and, theoretically, you shouldn't have any problems. But sooner or later you will have a crash or forget the anti-seize and you will be in trouble.

To get home after a crash, bent stems can usually be straightened if you hold the front wheel between your legs and twist the handlebars. If one side of the handlebars is bent, lay the bike on the ground, place one foot on the stem and pull hard. As always when straightening metal, it's best to exert a slowly increasing amount of force and not make a sudden wrench. If that doesn't work, try to lever the handlebars straight with a length of wood. Once the metal starts to move, don't stop pulling until it's straight. Don't ride any farther than necessary before installing new parts.

In a frontal crash, the top and down tubes usually bend, but it's usually the damage to the forks that stops you from riding back home. If you can straighten them with a piece of tubing or a large adjustable wrench, you will be able to get home safely.

There are various sorts of problems best left to professionals. A good bike shop can remove seized cranks, straighten bent cranks and extract a corroded seat post. They should also be able to check and correct frame alignment, organize a respray for a frame looking past its best and clean up any damaged threads. If you are installing a cartridge bottom bracket, some people say you should get the bottom bracket threads recut as a matter of routine. On the other hand, a machine shop or car repair shop would probably be better at dealing with seized nuts and bolts.

Dealing with stuck parts

1 Alloy seat posts can corrode and jam in the frame. If you suspect this has happened, remove the seat bolt and apply penetrating oil around the bottom of the seat post every few hours for a couple of days. Then try again.

2 The best way of getting a grip on a seat post is to bolt on an old saddle. Hit it with a mallet to try to move the seat post. If that doesn't work, try turning it with a long pipe wrench.

5 You always need a long wrench to take off pedals but if you can't move them, extend the wrench with a tube. However, one of the reasons why people have trouble is that they forget the left-hand pedal has a left hand thread.

3 When a crank or something similar gets stuck, cushion it with cloth and strike the bottom bracket end several times with a hammer. If that doesn't shock it off, try riding a couple of miles with the crank bolt missing.

4 When somebody has tried undoing the wheel nuts with a wrench or used the wrong wrench on the rear derailleur, it's best to undo the damaged nut or bolt with a surface drive socket. These grip the sides of the hexagon, not the vulnerable angles.

6 Don't use too much leverage as there is a danger that you will rip the thread out of the crank. Instead, try soaking the threaded part in spray lube. Don't forget the end of the axle where it shows on the inside face of the crank.

7 Sometimes the wrench flats on the pedal axle get damaged. If that happens, dismantle the pedal and clamp the axle in a vice. Then pull on the chainring to unscrew the pedal axle but check you are turning in the right direction.

SAW POINT

If you are desperate, you can sometimes remove obstinate components using a hacksaw. In most cases you will find the junior size best. Put in a new blade before you start as that will make the whole job much easier.

Where something is held in place with a nut and bolt, slip the saw blade in behind the nut and cut through the bolt. If it's very tight for space, you will find yourself cutting through the back of the nut as well but that doesn't matter. If you are dealing with something like an anchor bolt with a damaged Allen socket, cut a deep slot across the socket head and try undoing it with a screwdriver. If you've good access to a nut, try making two diagonal cuts across opposite flats. Then open up the slots with a cold chisel and hammer – the nut will usually fall apart. If all else fails, see if the local auto repair shop can help with specialist equipment.

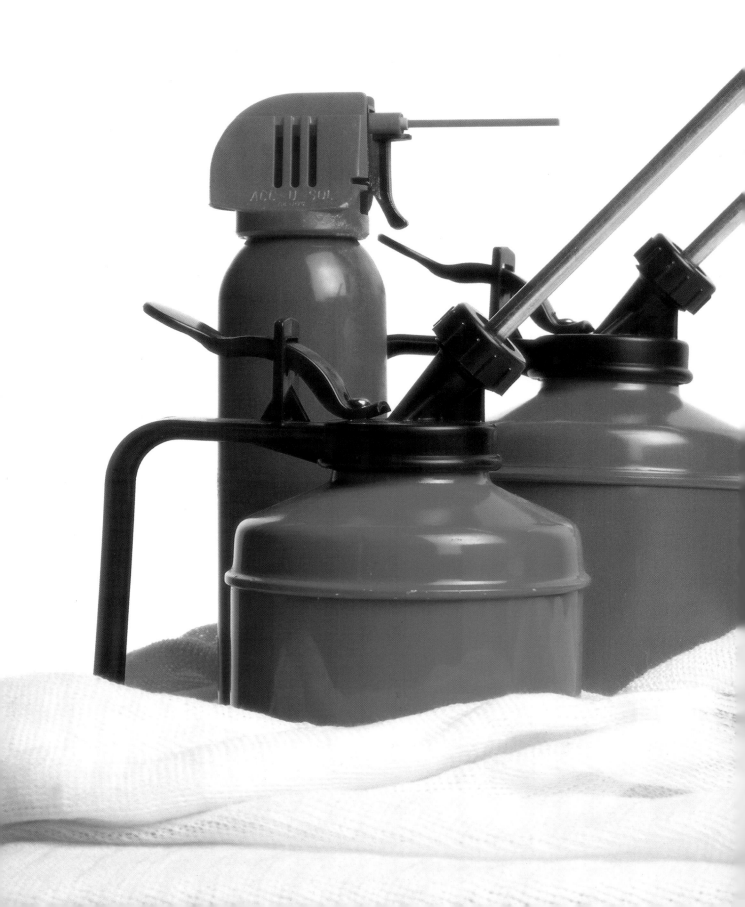

CHAPTER 3

INSTANT BIKE CARE

Bikes are best when they are looked after – gears change better, chains last longer, very little falls off. This chapter contains all the information you need to make sure your bike runs as it should.

Quick lube routine

You can't over-lubricate a bike. If it is swimming in oil, the worst that can happen is that it will pick up a bit more dirt than usual.

As they whiz around, chains tend to throw off any oil you put on them. They also get covered with dust and any oil that clings on gets washed off eventually. But if a chain is allowed to run dry, the chain, chainring and sprockets all wear out fast and derailleur gear systems will hardly work at all. The way to prevent this is to lube the chain frequently and to clean it as soon as dirt and dust start to build up on the links. Full instructions on cleaning chains appear on page 70.

For regular commuters, frequently means once a week in winter, maybe once every two weeks in summer. You should back this up with extra lube for the chain if it has been raining. Leisure riders should lube their bikes after any off-road trip and soon after any ride over 40 miles on the road.

That leaves the question of when to lube the rest of your bike. If you use this schedule and go through the whole lube routine every time your chain needs attention, your bike certainly won't be under-lubricated.

Try to fit this lube routine in with cleaning and checking your bike over mechanically.

1 Brake pivots are assembled with grease but need a shot of spray lube to keep water and rust at bay. Don't let it get on the pads or rims as it is difficult to clean it off.

2 Pulley wheels don't pick up oil from the chain so they need a shot of spray lube fired into the center to keep them turning smoothly. Spray lube also cleans them up nicely.

3 Rear gear mechanisms need a shot of lube on each of the main pivots, the top pivot and the chain cage pivot. In other words – if it moves, spray it. Then wipe lightly.

4 The front derailleur needs a squirt on all eight pivots, then a quick wipe around the chain cage. Lube the gear shifters and any point where the inner cable turns a corner.

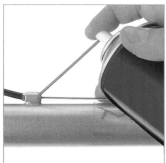

5 The chain must first be soaked with spray lube. Give it time to penetrate, especially if it contains a solid lubricant. Then give it a coating of heavy oil to back it up.

6 Brake levers need a shot of lube on the pivots. You should also pull back the brake lever so you can lube the brake cable. Don't leave the nipple dry or the cable may fray.

7 The front brake pivots also need a shot of lube. At the same time, inspect the brake pads for wear and, more important, check that they are correctly aligned on the rim.

8 All cables need lube. You can just give the inners a squirt where they exit from the housings but it is better to remove the housing from the stop and fire lube down it.

Big cleanup

Mountain bikes always need a good scrub down after a muddy ride but any sort of bike looks brighter after a thorough wash and polish.

The obvious thing to wash your bike with is dish detergent. That's fine if the bike is really oily because the detergent will strip most of the oil off, along with any wax or polish on the frame. But when it dries, the frame will probably look streaky because of the phosphates left behind. You will have to shine it up with car polish if you want to put the gleam back. If you find areas where the dish washing liquid isn't cutting through the dirt, apply degreaser, agitate with a brush and then wash again.

If your bike is just normally dirty, you might do better to wash it with car shampoo as that is generally less aggressive. It also leaves a film of wax polish, so your bike will certainly look better than it would after a dousing in dish washing liquid.

Try to avoid washing your bike in the sun as the heat will dry the frame too quickly, increasing the chances of streaks. Don't ever use a pressure washer because the bearings are not designed to keep out water under pressure. You can use a hose but keep the pressure down and don't squirt it directly at the hubs, bottom bracket, gears or headset.

Cleaning kit

SPRAY LUBE

DEGREASER

DISH WASHING LIQUID

500 ml

1 Squirt plenty of dish washing liquid or some car shampoo into half a bucket of warm water. Apply a first coat to the whole bike using an old sponge or dish washing brush but give it time to work.

2 Wash the whole bike again. This second pass will remove most of the dirt, but there may be areas where the dirt is more stubborn. Use a bottle brush to get into the nooks and crannies.

WHEN YOU NEED TO DO THIS JOB
◆ After an off-road ride.
◆ Every two or three months.

TIME
◆ Half an hour to do the job properly; 10 minutes if you're in a real hurry.

DIFFICULTY
◆ Dead easy. There is no excuse for not keeping your bike gleaming.

SPECIAL TOOLS
◆ Bottle brush, dish washing brush, toothbrush, close-textured sponge, chamois leather.

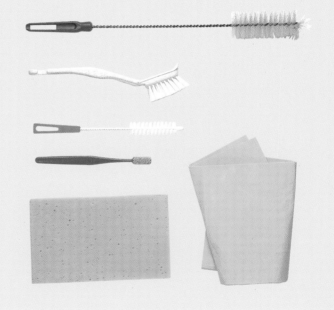

3 If there are areas where the foam seems to form droplets and roll off, give them a squirt of degreaser to break down the film of oil. Use an old toothbrush to ensure the dirt mixes with the degreaser.

4 If you've plenty of time, get a bucket of clean warm water and rinse the foam away. Use a sponge to cascade water over the frame and the mudguards but use it gently or it will get torn to pieces.

5 Dry the frame, mudguards, saddle and handlebars with a clean rag or a chamois. Then squirt spray lube over areas like the gears and the hubs where water might penetrate the mechanism.

WASH, LUBE AND GO
When you've finished washing your bike, even if you've dried it quite carefully, there is still a chance that water will have got into the bearings. On the other hand, if you oil your bike without washing it, there is a chance that dirt will get into the bearings. So treat washing and lubing as two parts of the one job and allow about an hour for the combined effort.

10-minute bike check

This routine will help you assess whether your bike is in good enough shape for daily commuting or a ride in the country.

1 If the brakes are properly adjusted, they will be fully on by the time you've pulled the lever about halfway to the handlebars. It is a danger signal if you can pull the brake lever any closer than that.

The first three steps in this test routine cover the brakes. If you find any defects in this area, don't use your bike until you've tightened the cable adjustment, installed a new cable, replaced the brake pads or done whatever else is necessary. Because the other problems don't represent a hazard, you can ignore them, if you wish, and risk damaging the bike or having to walk home.

Ideally, do your 10-minute check before the Quick Lube routine but after the Big Clean-Up. That way you will be able to handle the bike without getting dirty or oily but don't forget to lube it when you've finished the checks.

Next come checks on steering. It will be fairly obvious if anything is out of line but not so easy to tell if the headset is loose or worn. If it is bad, you will hear and feel a jolt when you lunge the bike forward and then apply the front brake. But if there is only a little slack, you might be able to detect it if you wedge your finger between the frame and the fork. Adjust or replace as soon as possible because loose headsets wear fast.

The chainset comes next. If you can detect movement on just one crank or the cranks feel tight or gritty when you turn them, it is best not to ride until you've fixed the problem. It is OK to ride with a loose bottom bracket but it will slow you down – so will a bent chainring, bent cranks and stiff pedals.

Gear cables tend to fray in the same places as brake cables, but they also fray under the bottom bracket on road bikes. However, badly adjusted rear gear mechanisms are the main cause of unreliability on nearly all bikes. So check that there is a quick reliable change between all gears. If the chain jumps off at any point, you will have to adjust the rear derailleur from scratch. Check the indexing as well – changes should be crisp and instantaneous.

Finally, check that the bolts on the saddle clamp, the seat post binder bolt and the handlebar stem are all tight. There is no need for them to be super tight, just tight enough to prevent the stem and the saddle from slipping out of position.

6 Grasp the pedal ends of both cranks and try to move them sideways. When they will move an equal amount to the left and the right, it indicates that the bottom bracket is loose.

2 Even if the brakes are correctly adjusted, check the brake pads next. There should be plenty of rubber left and at least 1 mm (1/32 inch) clearance between the pad and the top edge of the rim.

3 Brake cables usually fray near the cable adjuster or at the point where they emerge from the outer cable. Check both and make sure that it takes only normal pressure to apply the brakes.

4 After checking stem and handlebars for cracks, ensure that the handlebars are level and the stem lines up with the front wheel. Then apply the front brake and see if there is any play in the headset.

5 Hold one of the cranks still with one hand and see if you can move the other one. Then switch. If you feel even the slightest amount of movement on one crank, the crank bolts need tightening.

7 Lift the chain off the chainrings so you can turn the cranks freely. If necessary, take out the back wheel to give you enough slack in the chain to pull it clear. Then rotate the cranks to see if the bottom bracket needs greasing.

8 Using an Allen key, check that all the chainring bolts are tight. At the same time, look down from above to see if the cranks and the chainrings are both straight. Finally, make sure the pedals revolve freely, without any cracking noises.

9 On rear derailleurs, check the cable for fraying near the cable anchor bolt and wiggle the rubber pulleys to see if they are worn. Shift from top gear to bottom and back a few times to check that the gear change is swift and accurate.

10 Inspect the front derailleur cable for fraying, be sure the chain cage is parallel to chain. Then check that there is a 6 mm (1/4 inch) gap between chain cage and chainring. The change should be quick and reliable.

11 Finally, make sure that the saddle clamp and seat post clamp bolts are tight. Do not overdo it in case you damage the threads. Now turn the page for the checks on wheels and tires – the most important parts of any bike.

Wheel and tire servicing

Use this 5-minute check over the wheels and tires together with the 10-minute check over the rest of the bike on the previous page.

When you spin the front wheel, it should keep on turning for quite a while. There shouldn't be any kind of grinding or cracking noise. If it seems to slow quickly or you can hear odd noises, the hub probably needs stripping and greasing. And as it turns, it will be obvious whether the wheel is running straight or there is a problem. If it seems to wander from side to side, try to see whether the tire or the rim is out more. No tire is absolutely straight but a rim should be true to about 1/32 of an inch or less. Check also for the rim moving up and down.

If you've come to the conclusion that the rim is buckled, either from side to side or up and down, the instructions on page 126 may help. If the tire is more out of true, it may just be that the beads are not fitted evenly. On the other hand, the tread of the tire may be crooked or there may be a bulge in the sidewall. In both these cases, the only solution is to fit a new one.

All the spokes in a wheel should be at roughly the same tension. If there is a buckle, some of the spokes will probably be loose, but if they all seem to be slack, the wheel needs re-tensioning.

When you're checking the tire tread for small stones, look also for sponginess, deep cuts and an excessive number of stones. If there are more than a dozen or so stones, the tire is coming to the end of its days.

5-minute tire and wheel check

1 Lift the front wheel off the ground and give it a spin. If things aren't running straight, try to see if it is the tire or wheel that is out. Then turn the wheel slowly and use the brake pads as a fixed point to gauge how bad the buckle is.

BUBBLE TROUBLE

If a tire keeps deflating, but you can't find the puncture, the valve may be allowing air to escape. This will show up if you remove the tube and dunk it in water, but there is a way of checking without going that far. Just fill a small bowl with water and dip the valve in. If there is a stream of bubbles, you will have to put in a new tube if it is a Presta valve, or a new insert if it is a Schrader.

2 If the tire isn't running straight, take it off and re-fit it, making sure the beads fit into the well properly. Then, whether it is buckled or not, stretch each pair of spokes with your finger and thumb to see if they are correctly tensioned.

3 Go around the tire with a small screwdriver next, prying out any stones stuck in the tread. Look out for deep cuts, whether or not there is a stone embedded in them, and consider buying a new tire if there is any serious damage.

4 The tire wall should be evenly colored, with an unbroken coat of rubber all the way from the rim to the tread. If the fabric is showing or there are any cuts or splits, deflate the tire so you can see how bad the damage is.

5 Finish the wheel check by turning the axle with your fingers. It should feel smooth, but, if it feels tight or gritty, disassemble and regrease. If it feels smooth, lay the wheel flat and run a few drops of oil between the axle and hub.

Inflating tires

1 To pump up a Presta valve, undo the knurled nut and push in the stalk until you hear a quick hiss of escaping air. This ensures that the valve is not stuck, but you may have to undo the nut a bit more if it's hard to force air into the tire.

2 A few mountain and utility bikes have a Schrader valve, which is a bit fatter than a Presta. Some pumps fit both types but you may need an adaptor, so check. Don't use garage air lines on Schrader valves – it's dangerous.

3 Most pumps just push onto the valve but the air will escape if you push the adaptor on too far. If you're having trouble, check that the adaptor is square onto the valve and steady your hand with a finger around the valve or a spoke.

4 When you've fully inflated a tire with a Presta valve, check that the valve is at right angles to the rim. Check also that the securing ring is finger tight. Don't overtighten it as that might cause a puncture. Then replace the dust cap.

10 hard-to-spot problems

After doing the 10-minute bike check, you should have enough know-how to spot all the common problems. This page will help you pick out the more unusual ones.

The 10-minute bike check will tell you if your bike is basically sound or not. But it won't help you trace the minor problems that make the difference between a bike that is just OK and one that is a pleasure to ride. Once you've spotted one of the problems outlined here, read the section covering that area to get a better idea about what action is needed.

First of all, don't neglect your riding position. Most people just get the saddle height roughly right and leave it at that. They forget the other saddle adjustments, the possible need to install a different saddle as well as adjust for arm reach.

But the biggest source of problems is the gears. If they are not working properly and minor adjustments don't fix things, go back and rework the adjustment from scratch. If that doesn't work, you will have to install a new chain and sprockets and possibly new chainrings and a new derailleur.

You may also have to splurge on some new tires. Just because there is $\frac{1}{32}$ of an inch of tread left, it doesn't mean that the tire walls are in good condition. If you check them, you may be left wondering why you don't get a puncture every time you go out. Putting on good-quality tires is the easiest and best upgrade for any bike – you will even go faster if you keep them properly pumped up.

The better the bike, the more likely it is that you will come across various creaking noises, because they are caused by different metals rubbing together. Don't try to eliminate them by overtightening bolts because there is a chance you will rip the thread out.

Brakes next. Again, just because there is a $\frac{1}{32}$ of an inch of rubber left on the pad, it doesn't mean that the pad is gripping the rim properly. Install new ones if the rim or pad feels slippery and adjust them either parallel with the rim or slightly toed-in towards the front. The new pads may well have instructions covering this point. But don't expect the new pads to generate full power immediately – they usually have to lay a coating on the rims and wear into the shape of the braking surface before they reach full stopping power.

Finally, there are the forgotten bearings. If a bike is getting on a bit, you may well find that these components are just worn out.

1 Too much effort needed, lack of comfort and a feeling of poor control over the bike can all be caused by a bad riding position. Go back to the recommended basic position and work from there.

2 The chain is worn if you can almost lift it off the chainring. It won't cause clear-cut problems but the chain-rings and sprockets will wear fast and the gear change will be sloppy and inaccurate.

5 Tires may look good from a distance, but it takes a close examination to get at the truth. If a tire wall looks worn, try letting the tire down so you can squeeze it flat and check for splits and cuts.

6 Bikes should be silent. If yours creaks, the noise probably comes from steel bolts in alloy threads or vice versa. Apply anti-seize to the stem, chain wheel and saddle bolts to silence them.

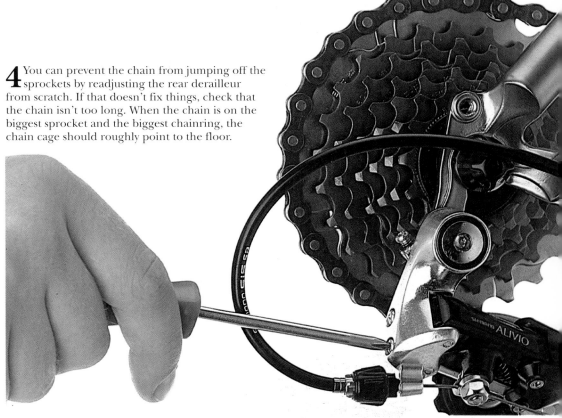

4 You can prevent the chain from jumping off the sprockets by readjusting the rear derailleur from scratch. If that doesn't fix things, check that the chain isn't too long. When the chain is on the biggest sprocket and the biggest chainring, the chain cage should roughly point to the floor.

3 If there is a regular noise that stops when you stop pedalling, the indexing on the rear derailleur is probably not working. Try turning the cable adjuster on the rear gear one half-turn counterclockwise.

7 Poor braking may be due to contaminated brake pads. Try installing new ones. Oil or grease building up on the rim also impairs braking. Remove with alcohol or scrub rims with a nylon scouring pad.

8 Badly mounted brake pads can cause grabby, noisy brakes, especially if each pad is aligned differently. Try installing so that the front edge is $\frac{1}{32}$ inch closer to the rim than the back edge.

9 Chattering brakes can be caused by a badly adjusted headset. Wrap your fingers around the bottom race and put the front brake on. If you can feel any movement, the headset must be looked at.

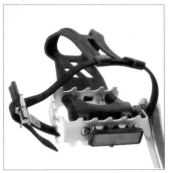

10 Pedals with grinding bearings or bent axles make it impossible to pedal correctly. Check that the axle is straight by eye, then remove from crank so that you can check the bearings.

43

CHAPTER 4

GEAR SYSTEMS

Where motorists see a flat road, bike riders see climbs
and dips. When weather forecasters talk about a still
day, cyclists can feel a head wind. So every day and
every road are different, each one requiring a different
gear ratio to balance speed and effort.

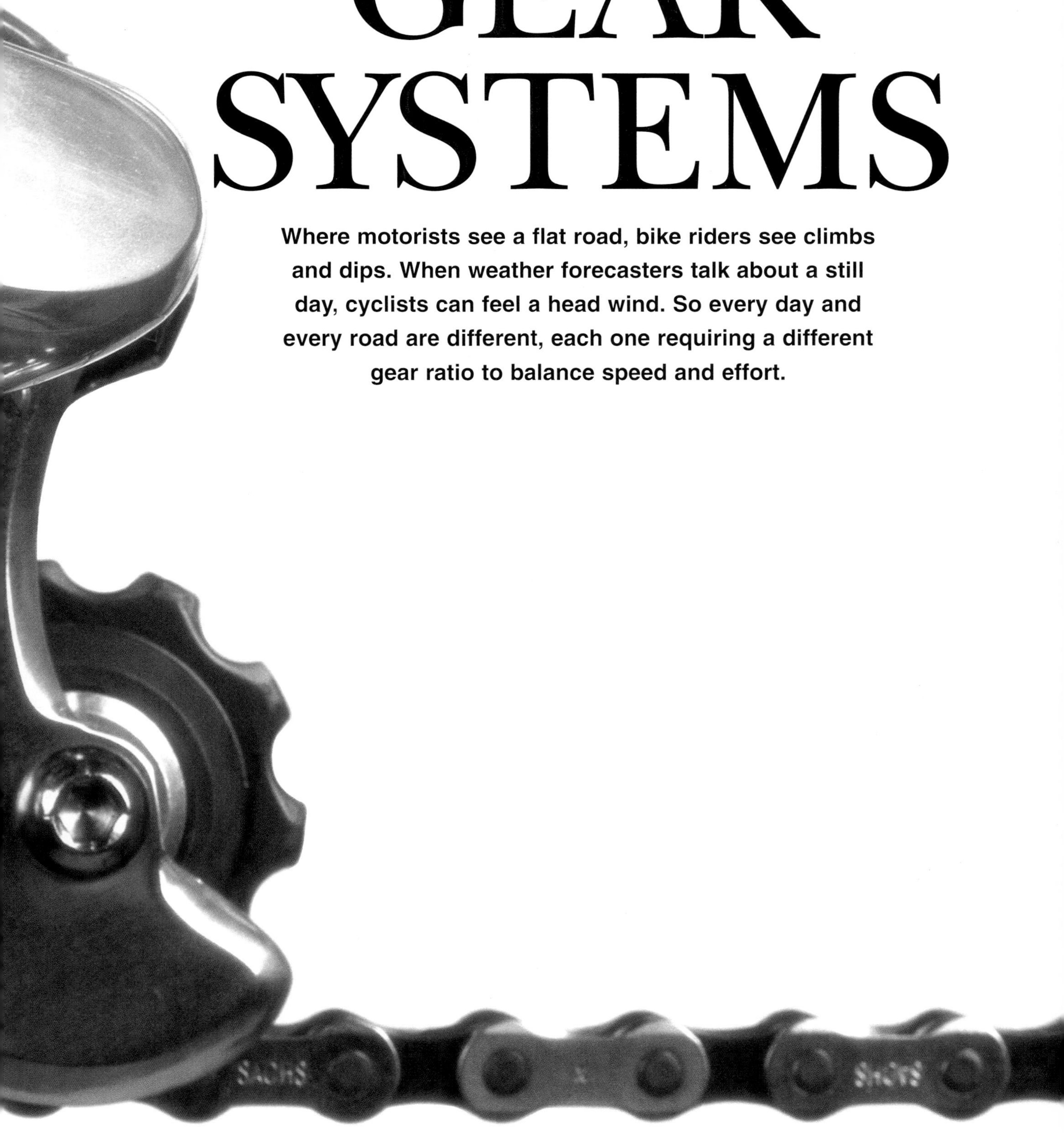

Types of gears

Nearly all bikes have either derailleur or hub (internal) gears. Derailleur gears have a front derailleur to shift the chain between two or three chainrings at the front and a rear derailleur for up to eight sprockets at the back. These gears need a lot of maintenance but they are light, efficient and suit most conditions. Hub gears have only three, five or seven speeds and need little maintenance.

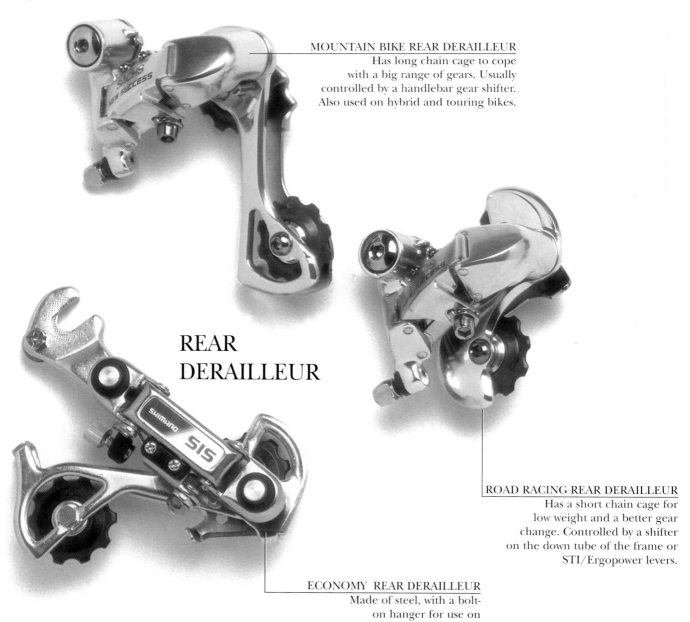

MOUNTAIN BIKE REAR DERAILLEUR
Has long chain cage to cope
with a big range of gears. Usually
controlled by a handlebar gear shifter.
Also used on hybrid and touring bikes.

REAR
DERAILLEUR

ROAD RACING REAR DERAILLEUR
Has a short chain cage for
low weight and a better gear
change. Controlled by a shifter
on the down tube of the frame or
STI/Ergopower levers.

ECONOMY REAR DERAILLEUR
Made of steel, with a bolt-
on hanger for use on
frames without a gear
hanger. Short cage
model also available.

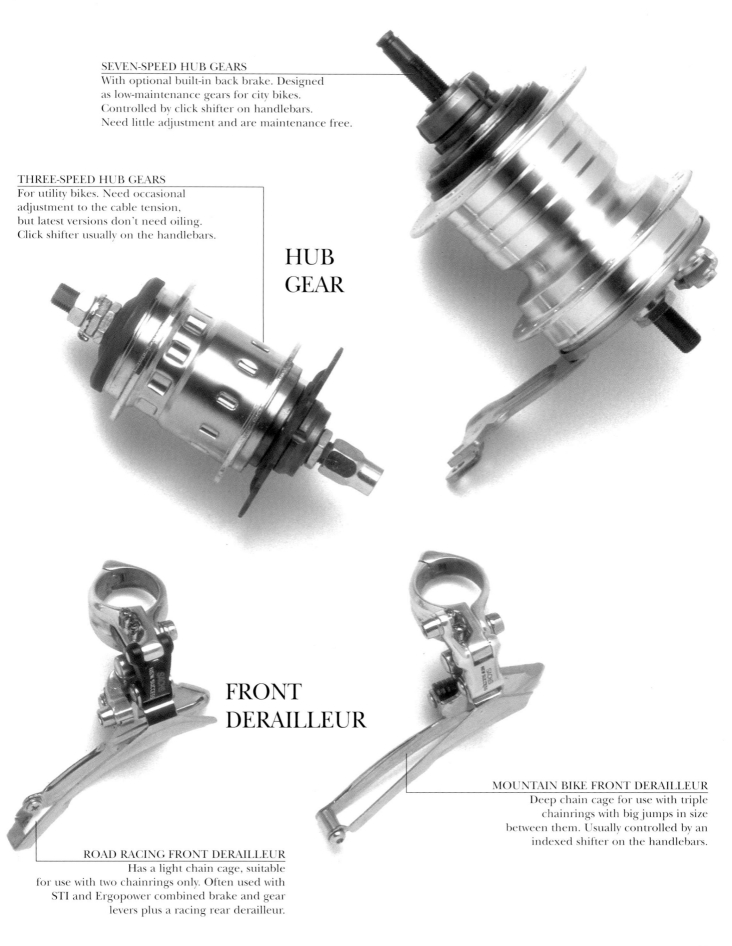

SEVEN-SPEED HUB GEARS
With optional built-in back brake. Designed
as low-maintenance gears for city bikes.
Controlled by click shifter on handlebars.
Need little adjustment and are maintenance free.

THREE-SPEED HUB GEARS
For utility bikes. Need occasional
adjustment to the cable tension,
but latest versions don't need oiling.
Click shifter usually on the handlebars.

HUB
GEAR

FRONT
DERAILLEUR

MOUNTAIN BIKE FRONT DERAILLEUR
Deep chain cage for use with triple
chainrings with big jumps in size
between them. Usually controlled by an
indexed shifter on the handlebars.

ROAD RACING FRONT DERAILLEUR
Has a light chain cage, suitable
for use with two chainrings only. Often used with
STI and Ergopower combined brake and gear
levers plus a racing rear derailleur.

Rear derailleur: care and inspection

When you're climbing a hill and the pedals are turning slower and slower, you need a quick change to a lower gear. That's when you'll find out if your rear derailleur is working properly.

The rear derailleur is the most important part of a derailleur gear system and needs regular lubrication and attention if you want it to deliver top performance. To find out exactly what maintenance is needed, you need to know whether or not the rear derailleur is indexed.

If you've got an older bike, it'll probably have friction gears. With these gears, you have to judge for yourself how far to move the gear lever each time you want to change gear. Nevertheless, once you've got the hang of it, each change should be crisp and should come in with one loud clonk.

On newer bikes with indexed gears, you'll feel and hear a click as you move the gear lever, along with a slight answering clonk as the chain jumps onto the chosen sprocket.

If either type of rear derailleur throws the chain off the sprockets, or you can hear the continuous metallic rattling sound of the chain trying to move onto the next sprocket but not quite making it, something is wrong. The first steps to fixing this are cleaning, lubing and adjusting, as explained in the next few pages.

Finally, remember that top gear is always the smallest sprocket and bottom always the largest. You therefore change up towards the small sprocket and down towards the big one.

1 If you've had to clean the chain, the rear derailleur prob-ably needs cleaning as well. Give it a squirt of aerosol lube or grease solvent and wipe it thoroughly with a cloth. Then lube all four main pivots, plus the top pivot.

2 Pay particular attention to the pulley wheels because they pick up hard-packed dirt off the chain. Soften the dirt with solvent and scrape off with a small screwdriver. Wipe, and then fire lube into the center of both pulley wheels.

4 Pulley wheels wear out fairly quickly. To check for wear, pull the chain cage forward to free the bottom wheel from the chain, then test for diagonal movement with your finger tips. Check also that the pulley wheel turns freely.

5 Pull the chain away from the upper pulley wheel and again check for wear and free movement. On recent derailleurs, the top pulley is designed to move sideways, so distinguish between wear and this intentional movement.

WHEN YOU NEED TO DO THIS JOB:
◆ Steps 1, 2 and 3 – every time you lube the chain.
◆ Steps 4, 5 and 6 – every time you give the chain a thorough cleaning. It's also worth going through 4, 5 and 6 when checking over a secondhand bike.

TIME:
◆ 1 minute to lube the rear derailleur when you do the chain; 5 minutes to check wear and crash damage.

DIFFICULTY: ╱╱
◆ Quite easy, but you are liable to get your hands pretty dirty. Consider wearing latex gloves.

NO SPECIAL TOOLS NEEDED

3 Gear cables should instantly transmit each movement of the gear lever. To ensure that this happens, lubricate the inner cables, then operate the gear levers a few times so that the lube works its way along the housing.

6 Hanging down beside the back wheel, a rear derailleur is quite liable to damage when a bike falls over, whether you're on it or not. To check for damage, clamp the bike in a workstand or get somebody to hold it upright. Then position yourself behind the back wheel, with your eye roughly level with the hub. From here you'll be able to see if the gear looks out of line with the frame. If you suspect that it is, check the gear hanger for signs of chipped paint – a sure indication that it's bent. Also check that the chain cage plates look straight. If all is well, the top and bottom pulleywheels will line up exactly with the sprockets.

DERAILLEUR HANGER

ANGLE ADJUST SCREW

TOP PIVOT BOLT

HIGH GEAR ADJUST SCREW

LOW GEAR ADJUST SCREW

CABLE ADJUSTER

CABLE ANCHOR BOLT

TOP PULLEY WHEEL

OUTER CHAIN CAGE PLATE

BOTTOM PULLEY WHEEL

SHIMANO ALIVIO

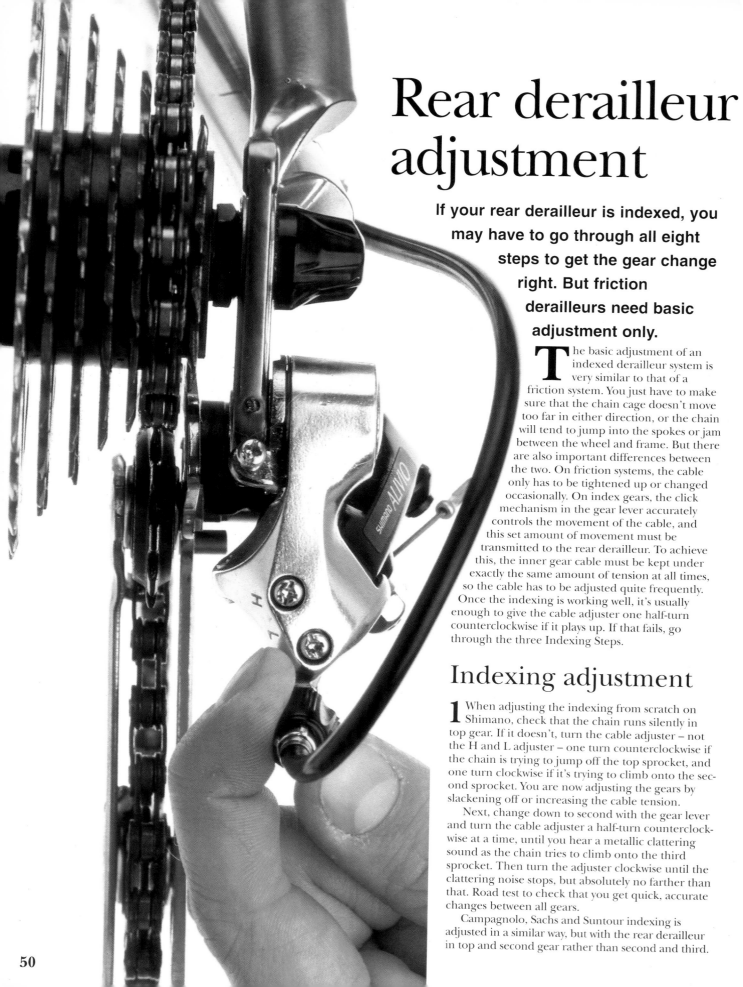

Rear derailleur adjustment

If your rear derailleur is indexed, you may have to go through all eight steps to get the gear change right. But friction derailleurs need basic adjustment only.

The basic adjustment of an indexed derailleur system is very similar to that of a friction system. You just have to make sure that the chain cage doesn't move too far in either direction, or the chain will tend to jump into the spokes or jam between the wheel and frame. But there are also important differences between the two. On friction systems, the cable only has to be tightened up or changed occasionally. On index gears, the click mechanism in the gear lever accurately controls the movement of the cable, and this set amount of movement must be transmitted to the rear derailleur. To achieve this, the inner gear cable must be kept under exactly the same amount of tension at all times, so the cable has to be adjusted quite frequently. Once the indexing is working well, it's usually enough to give the cable adjuster one half-turn counterclockwise if it plays up. If that fails, go through the three Indexing Steps.

Indexing adjustment

1 When adjusting the indexing from scratch on Shimano, check that the chain runs silently in top gear. If it doesn't, turn the cable adjuster – not the H and L adjuster – one turn counterclockwise if the chain is trying to jump off the top sprocket, and one turn clockwise if it's trying to climb onto the second sprocket. You are now adjusting the gears by slackening off or increasing the cable tension.

Next, change down to second with the gear lever and turn the cable adjuster a half-turn counterclockwise at a time, until you hear a metallic clattering sound as the chain tries to climb onto the third sprocket. Then turn the adjuster clockwise until the clattering noise stops, but absolutely no farther than that. Road test to check that you get quick, accurate changes between all gears.

Campagnolo, Sachs and Suntour indexing is adjusted in a similar way, but with the rear derailleur in top and second gear rather than second and third.

Basic adjustment

1 If you're adjusting friction gears, check that the center screw of the shifter is tight. On index gears (both down tube and handlebar shifters) ensure that the center screw or indicator is in the indexed position.

2 Check the inner cable is well lubed and isn't frayed, and that the housing isn't bent or broken. Select top gear position by moving the gear lever or, if Rapidfire, STI or similar, by clicking it at least 7 times.

5 The H (top) and L (bottom) adjusters are usually on the top pivot but on budget Shimano and most Camy gears, they are alongside the cable anchor bolt. In some cases they're not labelled H and L, and you'll have to experiment to find which adjuster is which. Now install the gear cable, pulling it taut with pliers before tightening the anchor bolt. Friction gears should be road tested at this point, and fine adjustments made to the H and L screws if the chain is noisy in either top or bottom gear. Index gears are now ready for adjustment to the indexing itself.

3 Undo the cable anchor bolt and turn the pedals until the chain jumps onto the smallest sprocket. Pull the derailleur into a vertical position and, from the back, check the position of the pulley wheels. If they are to the left of the smallest sprocket, turn adjuster H for High counterclockwise or, if they are too far to the right, turn it clockwise. On a friction gear, the pulley wheels must line up with the middle of the top sprocket. On index gears, the pulley wheels must line up with the outer edge of the sprocket.

4 Still working from behind, push the rear derailleur sideways with your right hand, then lift the chain onto the bottom sprocket with your left. The chain cage should line up with the middle of the bottom sprocket. If it doesn't, turn the L adjuster screw clockwise if the chain cage is to the left of the largest sprocket, and counterclockwise if it lies to the right. Now lift the saddle so you can give the pedals a few quick turns. The chain should quickly jump down to the smallest sprocket and stay there.

WHEN YOU NEED TO DO THIS JOB

◆ Rear derailleur is noisy.
◆ Gears won't change quickly, smoothly and accurately.
◆ Chain jumps off into spokes or gets jammed between sprocket and frame.

TIME

◆ 30 minutes from installing new derailleur to completing adjustment of indexed rear derailleur.
◆ 5 minutes to fine-tune the indexing, including test ride.

DIFFICULTY

◆ Basic adjustment is quite straightforward, but getting the indexing working perfectly can take patience.

NO SPECIAL TOOLS NEEDED

2 If the indexing still isn't perfect, or is having an off-day, fine-tune cable tension by turning the cable adjuster a quarter-turn counterclockwise, then clockwise. On most MTBs, you can do this with the cable adjuster on the shifter.

3 Racing bikes with STI and Ergopower usually have an adjuster on the frame that you can reach when riding along. As with twist-grip MTB shifters, this means that you can check out the indexing and fine-tune cable tension as you ride.

CHAIN CLASHES

There's a third adjuster screw on most rear derailleurs which you don't normally touch. But if you install a new cluster or rear derailleur, and there isn't room for the pulley wheel in top or bottom gear, screw in the angle adjuster screw until the chain runs normally.

51

Rear derailleur: overhaul and replace

If you've carefully adjusted your rear derailleur but still can't get the gears working nicely, it may need disassembling and cleaning.

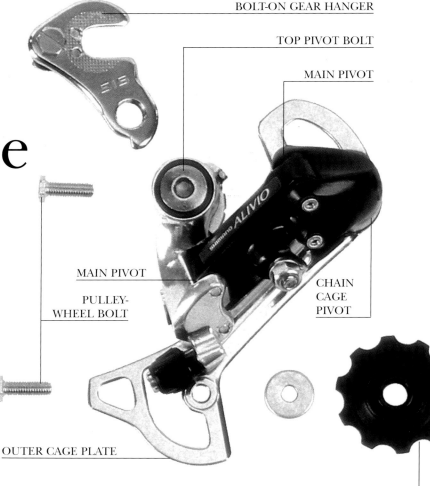

BOLT-ON GEAR HANGER

TOP PIVOT BOLT

MAIN PIVOT

MAIN PIVOT

PULLEY-WHEEL BOLT

CHAIN CAGE PIVOT

OUTER CAGE PLATE

BOTTOM PULLEY WHEEL

There's no set interval for stripping and cleaning a rear derailleur but if you're the kind of MTB rider who revels in mud, once a month is the minimum. On the other hand, road riders often go for years without touching the rear derailleur. That's leaving it too long and when the cable needs replacing, or you find that the pulley wheels are worn or won't turn freely, it's time for a strip-down, a thorough cleaning and possibly new pulley wheels. Some gears will break down into many more parts than are shown in the diagram, but there's no need to go any farther than separating the chain cage plates and stripping the pulley wheels.

While you've got the derailleur off, you should also check for wear in the main pivots. To do this, grip the top and bottom parts of the gear and try to move them in opposite directions. If you can, the main pivots are worn and a new derailleur is needed. One other check, on the bike, is to hold the bottom of the chain cage and see if it will move up and down. If it'll move more than about ¼ inch, check for wear in the top and chain cage pivots.

The method of removing a rear derailleur shown here avoids splitting the chain and should be used whenever possible. However, if you find that you can't remove the pulley wheels, you'll have to split the chain and then unbolt the rear derailleur. But remember that every time you split a chain, it's that little bit more likely to break at some other time.

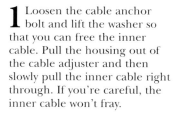

1 Loosen the cable anchor bolt and lift the washer so that you can free the inner cable. Pull the housing out of the cable adjuster and then slowly pull the inner cable right through. If you're careful, the inner cable won't fray.

2 Take out the bolt holding the bottom pulley wheel in the chain cage, and remove the pulley. As you do so, try to see where the various shaped washers fit. If the bolt won't move, soak both ends in spray lube and leave for a while.

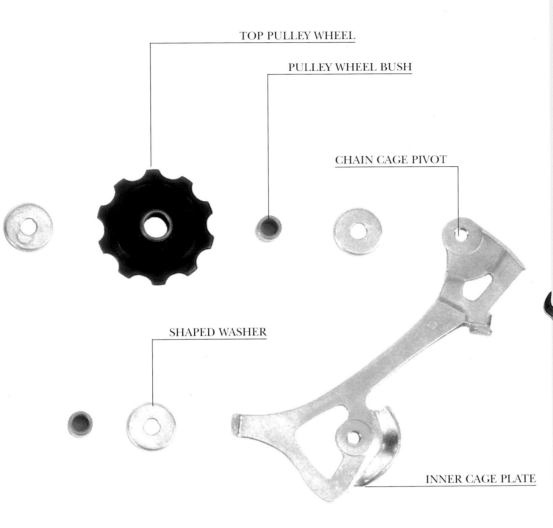

TOP PULLEY WHEEL

PULLEY WHEEL BUSH

CHAIN CAGE PIVOT

SHAPED WASHER

INNER CAGE PLATE

WHEN YOU NEED TO DO THIS JOB:
◆ Poor changing indicates derailleur needs cleaning.
◆ Inspection reveals pulley wheels are worn.
◆ Inspection reveals derailleur is worn out.

TIME:
◆ About 1 hour to remove, thoroughly clean and re-install a rear derailleur.
◆ 30 minutes to install a new derailleur.

DIFFICULTY
◆ It's sometimes hard to reassemble the pulley wheels correctly.

SPECIAL TOOLS
◆ It's very important to have a well-fitting wrench or Allen key to undo the pulley wheel bolts.

3 Loosen the top pulley bolt next, allowing you to swing the inner cage plate away. Then lift the chain and disengage it from the top pulley wheel. Move the chain onto one of the large sprockets and let the slack hang down.

4 The derailleur is now ready for removal. Pry off the plastic cover, or clean out the Allen key socket, and undo the pivot bolt with an Allen key. If the gear is fitted with a bolt-on hanger, loosen the screw and pull off the frame.

5 On the bench, undo the top pulley bolt and note how the washers fit. Clean everything in solvent, dry and re-assemble, oiling the pulley wheel bearings as you do so. Use anti-seize grease on the pulley bolts and pivot bolt.

6 Screw the pivot bolt into the hanger, tighten it hard and check that there is no play here. Lube all the pivots with oil, check that the pulley wheels align with the sprockets, then go through the whole adjustment process.

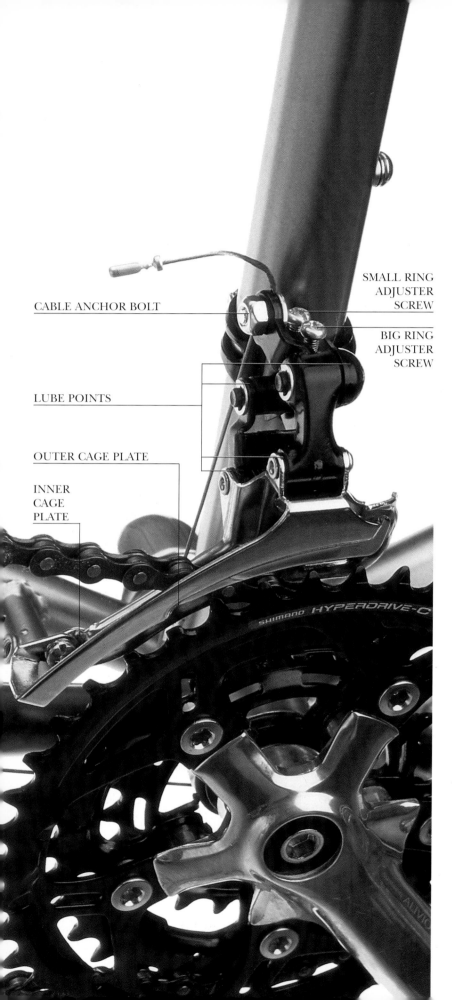

CABLE ANCHOR BOLT

SMALL RING
ADJUSTER
SCREW

BIG RING
ADJUSTER
SCREW

LUBE POINTS

OUTER CAGE PLATE

INNER
CAGE
PLATE

SHIMANO HYPERDRIVE-C

Front derailleur: care and adjustment

Front derailleurs are not temperamental like rear derailleurs – once set up, they go for ages before needing attention.

Front derailleurs all look roughly the same, so you must figure out which type you have. In particular, recent MTBs have an indexed front derailleur with a 1-2-3 indicator on the handlebars to make it easier to select between the three chainrings. But older MTBs and nearly all road bikes have a front derailleur that works with a friction gear lever.

The other main variation affects the chain cage. Triple chainring bikes usually have a big jump between the smallest and largest chainring, so mountain bike front derailleurs have a deep, heavily stepped chain cage. Double chainring road bikes usually have a smaller jump between chainrings, so front derailleurs with smaller, lighter chain cages are used. Don't try to make a front derailleur work on the wrong type of crankset, as it'll never be right. But with either type, the chain will sometimes scrape on the chain cage and that's perfectly normal. You just have to adjust the shifter lever a little as you ride along.

For maintenance, a front derailleur needs a quick squirt of lube on the pivots when you lube the chain, but apart from that the main thing is to clear any dirt that builds up on the chain cage. If you don't, it'll just transfer back to the chain later. It's also worth checking the chain cage and pivots for wear occasionally. But remember, front derailleurs wear out very slowly.

Watch out if you're working on a new bike, as some of the latest front derailleurs have adjusters that are in opposite positions from those on models that you may be used to.

1 Fit the chain onto the small chainring and screw the inner adjuster in or out until inner chain cage plate is 1 mm (1/32 inch) inside the inner chainring. Turn pedals to check adjustment.

2 Lift chain onto the biggest chainring. Screw the outer adjuster in or out until the outer chain cage plate is 1 mm (1/32 inch) outside the biggest chainring. Fine tune both settings on a test ride.

3 Indexed shifters have three definite positions. Select bottom on the rear derailleur and tighten or loosen the cable adjuster until the chain moves cleanly from the inner onto the middle chainring.

4 Front derailleurs with friction levers work best without any slack in the cable, so re-tighten after adjustment. If the front derailleur changes well but then loses adjustment, tighten center screw slightly.

5 If the chain won't climb snappily onto the outer ring, check that cage is parallel with chainrings and that outer cage plate is between 2 mm and 4 mm (1/16 to 1/32 inch) from teeth of the chainring.

6 If you have to move the front derailleur after checking its position, undo the cable anchor bolt and free the cable so it doesn't affect the position of the chain cage. Note route of cable through anchor bolt.

7 Slacken the clamp around the frame until you can move the front derailleur by finger pressure. Re-position the chain cage until it lines up with the chainrings and lies close to the teeth but not touching them.

FRONT DERAILLEUR ADJUSTER SCREWS
Sometimes the adjuster screws on front derailleurs are marked H = High = the biggest chain ring, and L = Low = the smallest chainring. This is similar to a rear derailleur, but the letters are often so small that it's very hard to read them. To identify which screw is which, just give the outer one an experimental half-turn and go from there.

Install new front derailleur

1 You can remove the front derailleur by first taking out the clamp bolt. Then pull the derailleur back and undo the Phillips screw or Allen bolt.

2 Pull the cage plates apart and lift out the spacer. Open up the gap and slip the front derailleur off the chain. Reverse procedure to replace.

WHEN YOU NEED TO DO THIS JOB
◆ If the chain jumps off when you are changing from one chainring to another.
◆ When fitting a new front derailleur.

TIME
◆ 10 minutes to adjust or remove the front derailleur.
◆ Another 10 minutes to check adjustment with a test ride.

DIFFICULTY
◆ Quite easy. In fact it's easier to work on a front derailleur than a rear. On the other hand, a front derailleur never changes quite as snappily as a rear derailleur.

NO SPECIAL TOOLS NEEDED

Gear shifters

Friction gear levers are easy to strip down but index shifters have many tiny parts and should only be opened up when really necessary. Twist-grip handlebar shifters should never be taken apart.

Nearly all mountain bikes have index gears controlled by shifters mounted on the handlebars. Only a few mountain bikes have friction levers and they just control the front derailleur, not the rear one.

Index shifters work either on a ratchet principle or a stroke principle. You can tell if it's a ratchet lever because there's a sharp click that you can feel and hear when you move the gear lever. Inside this type of lever is a round plate with a series of holes which represent each gear position. A spring-loaded ball bearing engages with the holes in the plate and creates the definite positions that you can feel as you use the lever. You should only take this type of lever apart if you can no longer feel the definite positions, or if it seems to have seized up and won't respond to soaking in silicone lube or something similar.

Stroke shifters are even more complicated. Although you can sometimes undo the tensioning bolt, remove the cover and then clean, lubricate with light grease and install new cables, you should never attempt to go any further. Where indicators are fitted, you usually have to remove two small screws to take off the indicator unit, then undo the central Allen screw, allowing you to separate the shifter from the brake lever.

STI and Ergopower road bike levers also work on the stroke principle and mustn't be taken apart. However, many road bikes have down tube levers, some of which are the friction type.

Friction levers can be stripped down without difficulty but they seldom give problems – disassembly is only necessary when they have become soaked in lube and you can't tighten the tensioning bolt enough to make them hold their adjustment.

1 Basic thumbshifter levers are found on budget mountain bikes. The large button at the front allows you to select friction gears if the indexing breaks down when you are out. They mount with a simple clamp.

2 Like most handlebar shifters, the only maintenance is an occasional spray with aerosol lube, then wipe clean. Try to direct the spray at the cable nipple, then operate the gear lever a few times.

OUTER PLATE

OUTER COVER

TRIM

TENSIONING BOLT

3 Rapidfire Plus levers have a separate lever for up and down shifts and mustn't be stripped down. To lubricate, remove rubber cap over nipple, if present, and direct lube into nipple recess.

4 Gripshifts and other twist-grip handlebar shifters are spring-loaded and inclined to burst open if you try to open them up. You can remove or adjust the position of a twist-grip shifter by loosening the Allen screw at the front.

5 Good quality road bikes may have two down tube levers. The front derailleur lever is nearly always friction while the rear derailleur often has an indexed lever. You can usually select index or friction by turning the tensioning bolt.

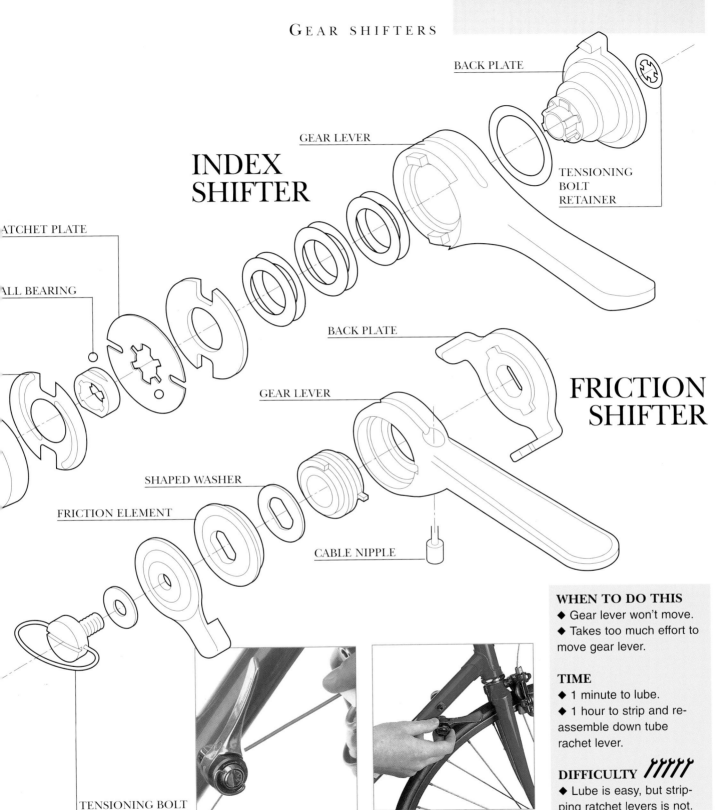

INDEX SHIFTER

BACK PLATE

GEAR LEVER

TENSIONING BOLT RETAINER

ATCHET PLATE

LL BEARING

BACK PLATE

GEAR LEVER

FRICTION SHIFTER

SHAPED WASHER

FRICTION ELEMENT

CABLE NIPPLE

TENSIONING BOLT

6 The cable fits into the lever on down tube levers, so don't direct the lube there. Instead, aim the lube at the edge of the central housing, from where it's more likely to find its way to the ratchet mechanism.

7 Most down tube shifters screw into bosses fixed to the frame, though a few are clamp-mounted. To remove, undo the screw and pull off. To replace, make sure you correctly locate the square cutout in the back plate.

WHEN TO DO THIS
◆ Gear lever won't move.
◆ Takes too much effort to move gear lever.

TIME
◆ 1 minute to lube.
◆ 1 hour to strip and re-assemble down tube rachet lever.

DIFFICULTY
◆ Lube is easy, but stripping ratchet levers is not. Most handlebar and twist-grip shifters are too complicated to tackle.

NO SPECIAL TOOLS NEEDED

Install new gear cables

When they become frayed or sticky with congealed oil, gear cables must be changed. Unfortunately there's a huge variety of gear shifters, so check the pages covering shifters first, then go through Steps 1 to 5 until you find the design nearest to yours.

1 Disconnect the derailleur end of the cable, then locate where the nipple fits into the shifter. On down tube shifters, move the lever fully forward and hold it while you push the nipple out of the recess. Use pliers to grip cable if necessary.

2 Handlebar shifters have a partly concealed cable recess. Try moving the lever into the forward position, then tracing the path of the cable around the lever. If you screw the adjuster right in, the nipple may pop out of the recess.

All inner cables look very similar but that can be misleading. So when buying, specify whether you have indexed gears or not. The high quality cables for indexed gears are stiffer than normal ones and both the inners and the housings are often specially treated to reduce friction. As a result, it's OK to use indexed cables on ordinary gears, but not the other way around. If you use non-indexed cables on indexed gears, it will affect the gear change and this means you'll have to adjust them frequently.

The next problem is that Shimano uses one type of nipple while Campy and Suntour use a slightly different one. So you also have to specify the make of gear and even then, you sometimes have to file the nipple a little until it fits snugly into the shifter.

When fitting new inner cables, always check the housings for kinks and breaks. If new ones are needed for indexed gears, use ready-made sealed housings from the gear manufacturers, or cut them yourself from the special housing cable made for indexed gears. This has separate wires running the length of the housing, held together by the plastic cover, so that it doesn't compress when the inner is fully tensioned. Ordinary housings are made of springy coiled wire, which does compress, interfering with the accurate transmission of cable movements.

Many cable anchors are designed so that the inner cable wraps around the anchor bolt slightly. There may be a curved slot to fit the cable in, but you should also make a mental note of the old cable path before removing the old inner cable.

Lubricate inner cables and housings with silicone, mineral oil and synthetic lubricants only. Never use grease or vegetable-based household oil.

3 On underbar setups, the inner cable fits into the shifter between the top of the gear levers and the handlebar. Gently pry out the rubber cap covering the nipple recess, where fitted. Select top gear and push nipple out of recess.

4 Underbar shifters sometimes have a cover held on by a central screw. Undo the screw and remove the cover, revealing the nipple and any cable guides. Pull the old cable out, fit the new one in its place, lube and re-assemble.

5 On STI levers, the nipple fits in the outer side of the brake levers and can only be seen when the brakes are applied. On Ergopower and Sachs levers, you have to peel the rubber hood back before you can see the nipple.

6 If the cable fits into an adjuster on the shifter, pull the housing out of its seat. Then slide a good length of inner cable through the gear lever so that you can feed it into the housing in a gentle curve.

7 Follow the route of the old cable with the new one. If you are re-using the old housing, make sure the metal ferrules are still in place and that the cable forms a smooth curve.

8 With down tube shifters, the cables usually pass under the bike and fit into a plastic guide on the frame. Check that the guides are not damaged, then carefully uncoil the cable to prevent any kinks.

9 Make sure that the gear lever is in top and that the chain is on the top sprocket. Feed the inner cable through the cable adjuster, seat the housing and lift the anchor bolt washer so you can make sure the cable fits into its slot.

10 Check again that the housing is correctly seated in the adjuster. Pull the cable tight with pliers and then do up the cable anchor bolt. Finally, cut off any spare cable with cable cutters and put on a cable end to prevent fraying.

WHEN YOU NEED TO DO THIS JOB
◆ If the cables are frayed or are sticky in the housing.
◆ When there's a mysterious problem with the indexing.

TIME
◆ 30 minutes to fit a rear derailleur cable, less to install a front derailleur cable.

DIFFICULTY
◆ It's easy to put new cables on a racing bike with down tube shifters, but handlebar shifters are tricky. It's very difficult to install new cables on a twist-grip shifter.

TOOLS
◆ A cable cutter is desirable.

METAL CABLE FERRULES

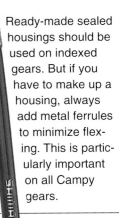

Ready-made sealed housings should be used on indexed gears. But if you have to make up a housing, always add metal ferrules to minimize flexing. This is particularly important on all Campy gears.

Sturmey Archer hub gears

Too many utility bike riders struggle along because their hub gears don't work. Yet they're the easiest gears of all to adjust and work really well in city traffic.

Inside all hub gears are a lot of carefully machined parts that have more in common with the automatic gearbox on a car than with anything else on a bike. Fortunately these internal parts seldom go wrong and on the rare occasions when there is a problem, it's probably due to wear and a complete new unit is usually the answer. The bad news is that you should never try to strip down a hub gear yourself, as it's unlikely that you'll ever get it back together correctly without special tools and know-how.

The commonest problem on a Sturmey is finding that you can only pedal in one gear – somehow you are in neutral when the gear lever is in other positions. The other big fault is slipping in the gears – there's a coughing noise and the pedals jerk. This happens more often going uphill and can be caused by internal wear. But this and every other fault are usually due to either incorrect adjustment of the cable, a broken cable or a broken control chain.

Follow the basic process given in Steps 5 to 7 to install new cables or control chains and to keep the gears in adjustment. New cables come complete with inner cable and housing and on older bikes, the housing is positioned with an adjustable heavy-duty frame clamp. If you ever find that you can't adjust the cable correctly, adjust the position of the frame clamp. And if the cable runs over a pulley, check that it turns freely.

The latest Sturmey Archers are sealed and don't need oiling, but if there's a black plastic oil port on the hub body, feed a few drops of medium-weight bicycle or motor oil into the hub every two weeks.

Wheel bearings are cup and cone type, adjusted in the usual way, but you'll probably need a special wrench. Adjust on the opposite side from the chain.

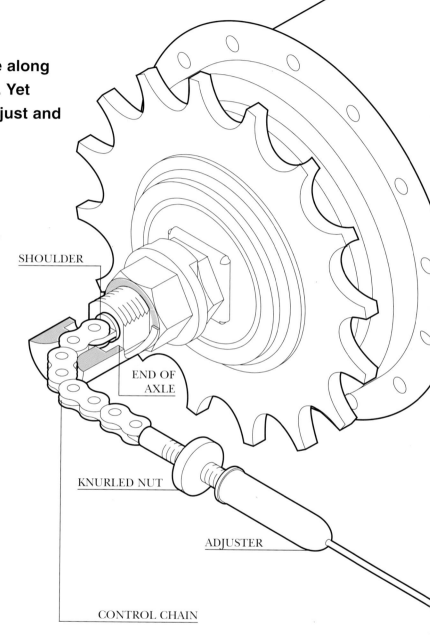

SHOULDER

END OF AXLE

KNURLED NUT

ADJUSTER

CONTROL CHAIN

Remove back wheel

1 On hub gear bikes, the gear cable connects with the back axle, so the first step is to separate them. Undo the knurled wheel on the gear cable one quarter-turn, then undo the adjuster about twelve turns to release cable.

2 Loosen both wheel nuts with a wrench, then undo them the rest of the way with your fingers. To prevent the axle from turning, special washers fit around the axle and into the frame. Place the wheel nuts and washers to one side.

3 Push the axle forward with your thumbs, but try to hold the wheel as it drops away to stop it from bouncing around. Now support the frame with one hand while you lift the chain off the sprocket and put the wheel to one side.

4 When re-installing, replace the shaped axle washers. Then do up the wheel nuts lightly, pulling the wheel back so that it is centered, with about ½ inch of play in the chain. Tighten the nuts, giving each side a turn at a time.

WHEN YOU NEED TO DO THIS JOB
◆ Cable is broken.
◆ Control chain is stiff or broken. ◆ Gears won't engage or slip (Step 3).

TIME
◆15 minutes to install new cable. ◆ 2 minutes for Step 3.

DIFFICULTY
◆ It's easy to fit a new cable, but adjusting the gears can be awkward.

TOOLS
Special cone wrench.

New cable and adjustment

1 Check first that the control chain moves freely and is screwed right into the axle. Undo it one half-turn at the most to align it with the control cable. If the chain is stiff or broken, simply unscrew the old one and screw in a new.

2 Put the gear lever into low and pry out the nipple of the old inner cable, then unscrew the housing from the back of the lever. Install new cable, bolt the cable at the correct length and tighten adjuster up to knurled nut.

3 Select N or 2 on gear lever and look through the inspection hole in the axle nut. Clean out if necessary. Move the adjuster up or down until the shoulder is exactly in line with the end of the axle. Lock with knurled nut, then test ride.

Torpedo and other hub gears

Torpedo hub gears are similar to Sturmey Archer but the new generation of multi-speed hubs is unusually complicated.

Torpedo hub gears are very straightforward three-speed units. Unlike a Sturmey Archer, they will always give you drive – you may not get the gear you want but at least you can always get one. The main thing that can go wrong is the cable. It'll either need tightening up or you'll have to install a new one. Use Steps 1 to 3 to help you with both these jobs. If you need to remove the back wheel, disconnect the gear cable as in Step 4, then use the procedure for removing a Sturmey wheel.

Shimano three-speeds are adjusted on the opposite side from other makes. First, check that the lever is working and that the cable is not damaged. Then select the middle gear showing N or 2 in the indicator on the lever. Turn the pedals backwards a couple of times and check if you can see the letter N in the window of the cable mechanism. If you can't, turn the cable adjuster until N is visible, then test ride in all gears. Fine-tune if necessary.

Five-speed Sachs, five-speed Sturmey and seven-speed Shimano hub gears are all quite complicated to adjust. You should leave them to a professional bike shop.

Most of these hub gears are sealed and don't need lubricating, but check with the supplying dealer if you're not sure.

Torpedo hub gears

1 Check that the control chain flexes easily and that it is screwed fully home into the axle. Also make sure that the cable is undamaged and isn't frayed where it goes over the pulley. Select H or 3 position on the gear lever.

2 The Torpedo cable comes in one piece, with a plastic ratchet that clicks on to the control chain. The length of the inner cable is adjusted with an Allen key via the cable bolt, so that the ratchet just reaches the control chain.

Sachs 7-speed hub gears

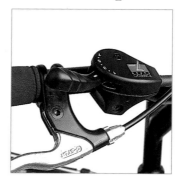 

1 If you suspect that the cable or lever on a seven-speed Sachs hub gear has been damaged, it can only be replaced as a complete unit. So undo the lever clamp, remove from the handlebars and undo all the cable fastenings.

2 There is no need to adjust the cable as it's sealed into the click box. This in turn fits onto the end of the axle. Occasionally loosen the mounting screw and push the click box onto the axle, re-tightening the screw by hand.

3 Bring the end of the control chain and the ratchet together, then push the ratchet onto the control chain as far as you can using minimum force. Check that the cable feels fairly taut but not under any tension.

4 Test ride bike in all gears. If you can't get all three, the cable is probably too slack. Press the chrome tab on the ratchet in with your finger tips to release it from the control chain, shorten cable slightly, re-connect.

3 Sitting on the end of the axle, a click box is quite vulnerable to damage when a bike falls over. Park your bike carefully to prevent this from happening and always install the guard when you replace the back wheel, just in case.

WHEN YOU NEED TO DO THIS JOB
- ◆ Control chain has broken or gone stiff.
- ◆ Cable has frayed or broken.
- ◆ You can't find all the gears.

TIME
- ◆ 10 minutes to install new cable on either Torpedo or Sachs 7-speed.
- ◆ 5 minutes to adjust Torpedo cable.
- ◆ 2 minutes to check click box location.

DIFFICULTY
- ◆ Very easy – much easier than adjusting Sturmey Archer.

NO SPECIAL TOOLS NEEDED

CHAPTER 5

CHAIN, PEDALS & CRANKS

The crankset is the heart of your bike, feeding the muscle power of your legs into the chain, which then transmits it to the wheels. It's this conversion of human energy into mechanical power that makes a bicycle so efficient.

CHAINRING

SPIDER

CRANK BOLT

CHAINRING BOLT

1 You mainly need to know the sort of cranks your bike has and the type of bottom bracket. Cotterless cranks are identified by the circular cutout where they bolt onto the bottom bracket axle.

CRANK

2 Standard bottom brackets have an axle that runs on separate bearing cups. Frequent stripping down and greasing is needed, as water tends to get in. These brackets are often identified by a toothed lockring.

TOE STRAP

TOE CLIP

REFLECTOR

PEDAL

Drive systems: components

Take a moment to identify the type of crankset and bottom bracket you are dealing with, before starting work. Cranks may be either cottered or cotterless; bottom brackets can be of a cartridge variety, or cup and axle.

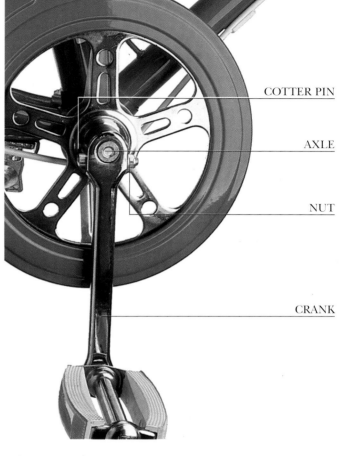

COTTER PIN

AXLE

NUT

CRANK

3 Some standard bottom brackets have a six-sided lockring and adjustable bearing cup to fit a large spanner. Others have two neat pairs of holes in the adjustable cup, to allow for a pin spanner.

4 Sealed bottom brackets have an axle that runs on two ball bearings inside a metal casing and seldom need any maintenance. There is no external lockring, so they look neater than a standard bracket.

5 Identify a cottered crankset by the cotters that run across the top of the cranks, locking them to the axle. They're nearly always made of chromed steel and fitted with a standard bottom bracket.

6 Standard pedals on most bikes accommodate running shoes, sneakers, or, better yet, bike touring shoes. On budget bikes and kids' bikes, the pedal bearings cannot be stripped down or adjusted, so consider upgrading.

7 Toe clips are vital to keep the ball of the foot over the pedal axle, which maximizes pedalling efficiency. The ultimate pedal is a spring-loaded clipless binding to clamp the shoe to the pedal; it's released by twisting the foot.

8 There are many designs of clipless pedals around. But they are expensive and only for serious riders, both on and off the road. They also require special shoes, and some shoe and pedal combinations don't work with each other.

Drive system: care and inspection

As the miles go by, wear gradually builds up in the drive system. To maintain maximum efficiency, check it over every few months.

If you keep the chain clean and well lubricated, you will slow down wear in the drive system by avoiding the most harmful cause of damage: the build-up of gritty deposits. Grit forms an abrasive paste with any oil or water around, so that every time the chain rubs against the teeth of the chainring or sprockets, a tiny fragment of metal gets worn away. Multiply that by the number of times the chain slips on and off the teeth of the chainring in 1,000 miles, and the amount of wear becomes significant.

Chainrings are usually made of soft aluminum. Luckily though, the action of the chain hardens the teeth, so that it's the steel chain and sprockets that end up wearing fastest. So fast, in fact, that after just a few hundred miles' use, the sprockets and chain are worn into each other. If you then try to run a chain on different sprockets, it probably won't mesh properly – there will be a regular cough or jerk, particularly when climbing a hill. The only way out of this is to replace sprockets and chain every time.

When the drive system is new, it wears quite slowly. But as the various components deteriorate, the rate of wear accelerates. If you replace the chain and sprockets before they're badly worn, you'll avoid the extra cost of having to buy new chainrings as well.

After you've been through all the checks, read further on in this chapter for details on maintenance or replacement, as required.

1 Most chainsets have separate chainrings, so the first move is to check that the bolts are tight. Sometimes the sleeve nut at the back of the chainring turns as you do so – try to hold it with a screwdriver.

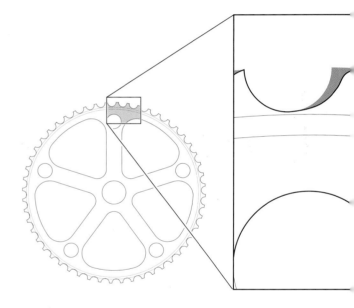

LOOSE CRANKS
If you find you can't tighten the left-hand crank far enough to stop it from moving, try filing or grinding a little metal off the reverse of the square hole, where it fits on the axle. Assemble with Loctite and tighten hard.

2 If the cranks are loose on the axle, they usually creak as you ride along. Test for looseness by holding one crank while you wiggle the other. If you can't get them tight, you may have to fit a new crank.

3 The next check is for wear or play in the bottom bracket bearing. Hold each crank near the pedal, and try to move them diagonally. If both cranks move the same amount, there's a problem.

4 Slip the chain off the chainring. Using the frame as a fixed point, turn the crank and see if the distance between the chainring and the frame varies. If it does, remove chainring and check spider as well.

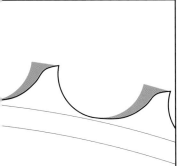

5 Inspect the chainring for wear next. First of all, the outline of each tooth gets blunted. By the time the teeth have become even slightly hooked, the chainring is well past it.

6 As chains wear, they also stretch, so measuring the length of a chain is a good way of gauging wear. Use a quality steel ruler as it is easy to read. Position the zero of the ruler on the center of a rivet.

7 Count out twelve links of chain. If the chain is new, the twelve links will measure 12 inches to the center of the rivet, while a badly worn chain, ready for the trash, will measure an extra ⅛ inch.

WHEN YOU NEED TO DO THIS JOB
◆ Every few months on a bike in regular use.
◆ When you're overhauling a neglected bike to bring it back into regular use.
◆ To assess how much you'll have to spend to recondition a secondhand bike.

TIME
◆ 15 minutes for a complete inspection, to include checking chain wear and chainline.

DIFFICULTY
◆ The hardest thing is distinguishing between the various possible problems with the cranks.
◆ It's also quite difficult to check the chainline with absolute accuracy, which is desirable on 7- and 8-speed bikes.

TOOLS
◆ Clearly marked steel ruler.
◆ A 500 mm steel straight-edge helps in checking chainline.

Chainline

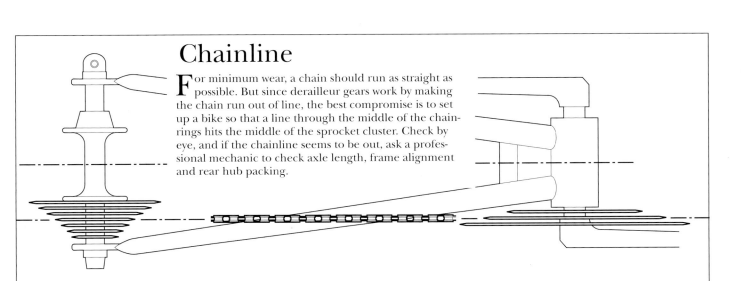

For minimum wear, a chain should run as straight as possible. But since derailleur gears work by making the chain run out of line, the best compromise is to set up a bike so that a line through the middle of the chainrings hits the middle of the sprocket cluster. Check by eye, and if the chainline seems to be out, ask a professional mechanic to check axle length, frame alignment and rear hub packing.

Chain: clean and lube

If you look after your chain, it'll transmit 95 percent of the power you produce to the back wheel.

Nearly all modern bikes have a chain ¾₂ inch wide. The only exceptions that you are likely to come across are kids' bikes and bikes with hub gears. These tend to have a chain ⅛ inch wide. The teeth on the chainring and sprockets match the width of the chain, so these components are not interchangeable between ⅛- and ¾₂-inch bikes.

If you're buying components for a bike that might have an ⅛-inch chain, look for the spring link and if there is one, tell the retailer that you need ⅛-inch components.

The instructions on these pages, covering cleaning and lubricating chains, apply equally to both types; but instructions about removing and replacing spring links are given on page 73.

If a bike has derailleur gears, it will have a ¾₂-inch chain, even if it is a kids' bike. These can only be split and joined back together with a special chain tool, apart from a few chains which have a patented joining link; but so far there are very few of these around.

Basic ¾₂-inch chains are most suitable for use with five sprocket clusters. More expensive ¾₂-inch ("ultra") chains are usually narrower and more flexible, so they work better on six and seven sprocket clusters. Bikes with seven and eight sprocket clusters should only be fitted with very flexible, high-quality chains, as they have to run a long way out of line. Even if you could get a cheaper chain to work, it wouldn't last long.

STIFF LITTLE LINKS

If a chain hasn't been lubed for a while, or you make a bad joint, one of the links may become stiff. This will probably show up as a regular cough or jump felt through the pedals. Sometimes you can loosen up a stiff link by pressing hard with your thumbs on either side of the rivet. But if the rivet sticks out more on one side than the other, fit the chain tool onto the side where the rivet sticks out farther, and push it in with a fraction of a turn on the punch.

Chain check

1 If you don't know which type of chain you're dealing with, clean the side plates and check the brand name. Sedis, Sachs and Taya are the commonest brands of standard chain. The rivets just push out and back in again.

2 Shimano chains are marked UG, HG or IG and the rivet heads are hammered over. When they're pushed out, the rivet holes become enlarged, and so special black joining rivets are used to join the chain up again.

3 When a chain has been neglected, some links stiffen up and cause a regular 'jump' in all gears. You can spot the stiff link by the kink in the chain, or because it feels stiff when you flex the chain. (See box above.)

WHEN YOU NEED TO DO THIS JOB
◆ Every month when the bike is in daily use.
◆ When the chain is visibly dirty.
◆ After a ride through mud or heavy rain.

TIME
◆ 15 minutes to clean a dirty chain; another 15 minutes to clean your hands. Consider using disposable latex gloves, obtainable from auto parts suppliers.

DIFFICULTY
◆ No special problems.

TOOLS
◆ Automatic chain cleaner, old toothbrush, lots of cloths.

Easy chain cleaning

1 If your chain is caked in mud, it's best to hose it clean. But if it's caked with oily dirt, you can remove the worst of the mess with a cloth. Make sure you wipe all four sides.

2 If the chain is dirty, the sprockets and chainring will be too. Use the edge of a cloth to get between the sprockets, and wipe the teeth of the chainrings as well.

3 The cloth won't reach inside the chain, so spray with solvent and scrub with an old toothbrush to deal with any grime that's left. Lay newspaper on the floor for drips.

4 When the chain is clean, lubricate first with a heavy oil. Let that soak into the rivets and then spray with an aerosol lube. Direct the lube at the sprockets so they get some too.

Chain wear

Chains wear quite fast, especially if they're not cleaned and oiled frequently. You can gauge wear by trying to lift the chain off the chainring. When both are new, you will be able to lift the chain only between 1 and 2 mm ($\frac{1}{32}$ to $\frac{1}{16}$ inch). The chain is due for replacement when you can lift it about 7 mm ($\frac{1}{4}$ inch); but remember, new sprockets must be installed at the same time in order to make sure that both parts mesh together properly.

Automatic chain cleaner

1 Automatic chain cleaners work best on derailleur bikes because they need slack in the chain. They scrub the chain like an old toothbrush, but don't work well if it's muddy.

2 Fill the chain cleaner with solvent up to the mark, hook the support behind the rear derailleur and then close the lid so that it hangs on the chain. Close the lid.

3 Slowly turn the pedals backwards. This will make the brushes revolve, scrubbing the grime off the chain. Repeat if necessary. Don't throw solvent away – put in a jar, and recycle.

Chain: remove and replace

Sometimes you simply can't avoid splitting the chain. But every time you do so, you increase the chances of it breaking unexpectedly.

When you're faced with a really dirty or rusty chain, try soaking it in paraffin or diesel oil, until it's as clean and flexible as new. This involves taking the chain off the bike, so the first thing is to identify which type you have (as shown on the previous page). Once you've done that, use the correct method of removal for your type of chain. If putting on a new chain, buy a ⅛- or ³⁄₃₂-inch replacement, depending on the size of the previous chain. If replacing a Shimano chain, don't worry too much about getting genuine Shimano, as other makes of ³⁄₃₂-inch chain work perfectly well with Shimano components. The only exception is the Shimano IG chain, which can only be used with all the other IG parts.

WHEN YOU NEED TO DO THIS JOB
◆ The chain is badly worn.
◆ The chain is rusty.
◆ You can't undo the pulley wheel bolts.

TIME
◆ Allow 20 minutes the first time you split the chain, as you'll need time to check each stage carefully.

DIFFICULTY 🔧🔧🔧🔧
◆ You'll have to use quite a lot of force to push out the rivet, which makes this job a bit nerve wracking until you're used to it. Also, when working on a Shimano chain you must be very careful to press out a normal silver-headed rivet, and never a black-headed joining rivet.

TOOLS
◆ Standard or Shimano chain tool.
◆ Hefty pliers and small file.

Standard chain

1 Wind the punch out and position the chain on the guides farthest from the handle. Shimano chain tools work on standard chains – you just have to adjust the support screw so that it presses on the back of the chain.

SHIMANO TOOL

Shimano Hyperglide chain

1 Select a silver rivet – never a black-headed one – to push out. Fit the chain onto the guides farthest from the handle, and adjust the chain roller so that it firmly supports the back of the chain plate.

2 Make sure the chain is seated securely on the guides. Wind the punch in until the pointed end hits the dimple in the rivet. Check that the punch is exactly centered, and then screw it in just under six full turns.

3 Try flexing the chain sideways to separate it. If it won't, push the rivet out another quarter-turn – but not right out. Try to leave a short length of rivet inside the chain plate, so you can snap the chain back together again.

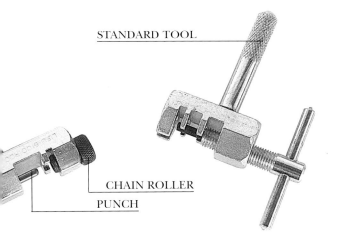

STANDARD TOOL

CHAIN ROLLER

PUNCH

Prying open ⅛-inch chain with master link

1 Utility bikes with ⅛-inch chains often have a chainguard to protect the chain from dirt. It's nearly always easier to take the chain off if you remove the chainguard first.

2 Turn the cranks until you spot the master link. Lift the tail of the spring clip off the head of the rivet with a screwdriver. Take care, or it'll fly across the room as you do so.

3 With the spring clip out of the way, take the loose plate off by flexing the chain, and then disconnect the fixed part of the spring link as well.

4 Re-join the chain by reversing the process for taking it off. The closed end of the spring clip must point in the direction in which the chain moves.

2 Check that the punch is centered, and then start pushing the rivet out. You'll probably be surprised at how much force is needed. Drive the rivet out, undo the chain tool and separate the two ends.

3 To re-join the chain, push the replacement rivet through the side plate into the chain roller. Slot the chain into the chain tool, then screw in the punch until it hits the exact center of the new rivet.

4 Remember, joining rivets install pointed end first. Don't ever split a Shimano chain unless you have a new rivet handy, as they cannot be re-used. They're usually sold in pairs so you have a reserve.

5 Push the new rivet in until you can see the groove around the rivet. Hold the chain with your fingers and snap off the bit that sticks out. If the rivet doesn't break cleanly, smooth with a file.

Thread-on freewheel

Thread-on freewheels have five or six sprockets. You'll find them on recent bikes in the budget price range, as well as nearly all older machines.

Sprockets (also called cogs) are the toothed devices attached to the back wheel. When five, six, seven or eight are combined together, they are called a sprocket cluster, or cluster for short. If the gear ratios on your bike aren't right for you, you can always install a new cluster with different size sprockets – but take advice on ratios that would work better.

With thread-on freewheels, the sprockets fit onto a separate body, which in turn screws onto the back wheel. The whole cluster gets changed when the sprockets are worn. Freehub sprockets fit into grooves on the freehub body. This is part of the hub and doesn't have to be changed every time the sprockets are replaced.

The two types look similar, but five- and six-speed clusters screw on, while seven- and eight-speed clusters are nearly always the freehub type.

WHEEL BEARING
LOCKNUT

Thread-on cluster

In the center of the cluster is a ring of cutouts into which the dogs of the remover fit. There's also a plastic spoke protector.

WHEN YOU NEED TO DO THIS JOB
◆ Sprocket teeth are worn.
◆ Freewheel needs cleaning in paraffin because action is noisy and gritty.

TIME
◆ Allow 15 minutes to remove a thread-on free-wheel, as it's best to take your time.

DIFFICULTY
◆ Take care – it's only too easy to damage the center of a sprocket cluster.

SPECIAL TOOLS
◆ Correct, undamaged freewheel remover.

Freehub cluster

Freehubs are sealed and have a longer life than thread-on freewheels. Details of removal are shown on the next page.

SPROCKET LOCKRING

KIDS' BIKES
To remove a single freewheel, position a blunt cold chisel in the recess in the center, and hit it with a fairly heavy hammer. The freewheel unscrews in the normal, counterclockwise direction. Take care not to cut into the center of the freewheel with the cold chisel.

Removing a thread-on freewheel

1 Undo the hub nut or the thumb nut on the quick release. Insert the remover into the body of the cluster, and carefully check for a perfect fit. If it's not right and you apply enough force to loosen a cluster, you'll wreck both.

2 Once you are satisfied that you have the correct freewheel remover, replace the hub nut or thumb nut finger tight so that it holds the remover in place. If you have a firmly mounted workshop vice, clamp the remover in the jaws.

3 With the wheel in the vice, turn the rim an inch or so counterclockwise. Alternatively, use an adjustable wrench to turn the remover about an inch counterclockwise. Loosen the hub nut a little, then unscrew the cluster a bit more.

4 Keep loosening the hub nut and the cluster bit by bit until it will unscrew by hand. When re-installing, use anti-seize compound on the threads and be careful: the thread is very fine and it's easy to cross-thread it.

Freehubs and sprockets

Seven- and eight-speed clusters can only be squeezed onto a bike by cutting down the width of the rear hub. Freehubs compensate for this loss of strength with a hub bearing fitted inside the sprocket cluster.

Freehubs pack a lot of functions into one small component, and you can only work on them if you buy at least three special tools. This isn't worthwhile unless you plan to change sprockets and freehub bodies frequently, so this might be a job best left to your local bike shop.

Bear in mind that on some early Campy and Suntour freehubs, the sprockets are held on with a threaded top sprocket. In this case, the top sprocket is unscrewed using two chain whips, or chain whip and removing tool. But both of these makers now use a lockring design, similar to the Shimano.

When assembling a freehub, it's vital to align the sprockets correctly with each other, as the ramps and cutouts on each sprocket work with the tooth profile on the next one to speed the gear change. Take note of whether there is one spline on the freehub body that is larger than the others. If so, and

you make sure that all the code numbers face outwards, you can't go wrong. You can confirm you've got it right by checking that the arrow on the side of the smallest sprocket points to the large spline. Freehub sprockets are also marked with a code number, and all the sprockets should carry the same one.

You may find that some of the largest sprockets are bolted or rivetted together. Sometimes you can open up these packs to change individual sprockets, but not always. In other instances there are separate sprockets and spacers. In either situation, take care to lay the components down on the bench in the correct order and facing the right way, so you can re-assemble them with minimum delay.

Lubricate freehubs occasionally, particularly when it's been wet. Do this by laying the wheel on its side, and filling the center of the freehub body with oil until clean oil drips out from the bottom.

CHAIN WHIP

Taking off sprockets

1 Take the back wheel out of the frame, then clean up the end of the axle and the smallest sprocket. Undo the thumb nut and also take the spring off the quick release.

2 Check that you have the correct removing tool. Fit the tool into the circular slot and hold it there by screwing the thumb nut back onto the quick release.

3 Position the chain whip on the bottom of the middle sprocket. Engage the long chain with the rest of the teeth, allowing you to exert force in a clockwise direction.

4 Fit a wrench on the lockring tool and apply force in the opposite, counterclockwise direction. It's best to steady the wheel on the floor with your feet as you do this.

Freehub body

1 Once you've removed the sprockets, take off the lock-nut and cone on the non-chain side of the wheel and pull the axle out through the hub. Take the ball bearings out of the hub, and wipe away any surplus grease.

2 You should now be able to see the six-sided socket in the head of the bolt that holds the freehub body to the hub itself. Check that the socket is clear and then undo the bolt. You will then be able to lift the freehub body away.

3 While the freehub body is off, clean the touching surfaces of the hub and freehub body with solvent. Then apply anti-seize grease to the inside of the freehub body and the retaining bolt. Re-assemble by reversing the procedure.

4 While the freehub is off the wheel, take the opportunity to clean all the sprockets thoroughly and flush the body out with solvent. Then oil with heavy mineral oil via the gap between the inner and outer bodies at the back.

WHEN YOU NEED TO DO THIS JOB
◆ New sprockets may well be needed if you are putting on a new chain.
◆ Different size sprockets may be needed if you go climbing mountains.
◆ The freehub body may need soaking in solvent or replacing if it won't freewheel.

TIME
◆ 15 minutes to remove sprockets.
◆ 10 minutes to strip out hub axle, if necessary.
◆ 5 minutes to remove freehub body.
◆ 1 hour to put everything back together again.

DIFFICULTY ✓✓✓✓✓
◆ One of the most difficult jobs you're likely to encounter on a bike. Removing the lockring is hardest, so your tools must be in good condition. Hub must also be re-assembled with great care.

TOOLS
◆ Appropriate lockring tool, in undamaged condition.
◆ Chain whip.
◆ Large adjustable wrench.
◆ 10 mm Allen key.

LOCKRING TOOL

5 It takes a lot of force to shift the lockring. Once it has moved, loosen the thumb nut and the lockring bit by bit, until you can undo the lock-ring with your fingers.

6 As the lockring unscrews, it makes a loud cracking noise – this is perfectly normal. Finally, lift all the sprockets off and lay them down on the bench as they come off.

Pedals: remove and replace

Don't underestimate the importance of your pedals. If they creak and grind as you ride along, you'll never develop a smooth and efficient pedalling style.

When they're doing the budget for a bike, makers often seem to leave the choice of pedals to last. This means that lots of bikes end up leaving the factory equipped with the cheapest possible pedals.

Common problems are that the cage breaks up or breaks away from the center, the bearings seize up and the dust cap falls off. You'll never be able to pedal efficiently with broken pedals. Above all they should be replaced right away as they're unsafe, and might pitch you off into the road.

Bearing problems often spring from careless assembly at the factory, when only a tiny amount of grease is applied to the bearings; and this soon gets washed away in the rain. So even if you've got a fairly new bike, it's worth removing and greasing the pedals as a routine precaution.

TOE CLIP

TOE STRAP

TOE CLIP/REFLECTOR BOLTS

PEDAL AXLE

BUCKLE

PEDAL CAGE
DUST CAP

PEDAL CAGE BOLT

LOOK FOR THE ALLEN SOCKET

Nearly all pedals have flats for a wrench on the axle. But some pedals also have a hexagon or Allen key socket formed in the end of the axle – easily spotted if you check the back of the cranks.

If you're working on pedals with an Allen key socket, it's usually easier to unscrew the pedals with a long workshop Allen key than with a wrench.

1 To remove the pedal on the chain side, fit a narrow 15 mm or 17 mm wrench onto the flats on the pedal axle. Undo in the normal, counter-clockwise direction.

WHEN YOU NEED TO DO THIS JOB
◆ If you are installing new pedals.
◆ When greasing pedals.

TIME
◆ 5 minutes.

DIFFICULTY
◆ The most testing part is remembering about the left-hand thread.

TOOLS
◆ Long narrow wrench or special pedal wrench, or long Allen key.

2 You may find it difficult to loosen the pedal. Try spraying the axle end with aerosol lube from both sides. Leave for a while and try again. If that doesn't work, turn the crank until the wrench is roughly parallel with the floor.

3 Hold the saddle and handlebars and put your weight onto the end of the wrench– be careful, as it'll probably move suddenly. If that doesn't work, use a length of tube to extend the wrench, and try once more.

4 Now for the left-hand pedal: this is very unusual in having a left-hand thread, designed to stop it from unscrewing as you ride along. You therefore undo a left-hand pedal by turning it clockwise – the opposite way from normal.

5 To make it easier to remove the pedals next time, coat the thread on the axle with anti-seize compound; or, if you have no anti-seize, some heavy oil. This is particularly important if the cranks are made of alloy.

CRANK

6 Check the end of the axle for markings. The left-hand pedal will be marked L or G; remember, it screws back in a counterclockwise direction. As you start screwing it into the crank, repeat to yourself, 'left-hand side – left-hand thread'.

7 It's awkward getting the thread started on a pedal, so support the weight with one hand while you turn the axle with your fingers. Finally, tighten with a wrench, or the pedals may start to unscrew as you ride along.

Pedals: overhaul

Though similar in principle to other bearings on a bike, pedal bearings can be surprisingly awkward to work on.

On any wet day, the pedals get showered with water. Most manufacturers try to combat this by fitting a rubber seal between the bearing and the end of the axle, but this isn't always effective. Nevertheless, when disassembling a pedal, you must take care to avoid damaging any rubber parts and to put them back in the exact spot that they came from. When the seal fits into the pedal cage around the inner bearing, it's sometimes useful to stick it in place with ordinary clear glue. It makes assembly easier and also prevents it from falling out in the future.

The other way to combat water is simply to use plenty of good quality, water-resistant grease. But once you've assembled and greased the pedal bearings properly, they shouldn't need attention again for many, many miles. Don't worry if the axle or cones are slightly pitted, as pedal bearings will still run smoothly with a certain amount of damage.

You will also find that smooth-running pedal bearings help you develop a good pedalling technique. There is no one pedalling style that works for everybody; but as a rough guideline, your foot should flex at the ankle at the top of its stroke, and be positioned roughly horizontal on the down stroke, which is when you put most of the power in. Some people keep the heel slightly below the horizontal, others keep it slightly above; variations depend on your own anatomy and the sort of riding that you do.

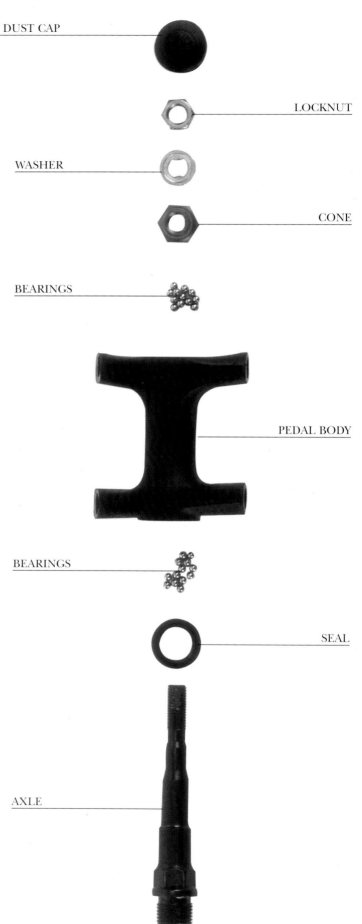

DUST CAP

LOCKNUT

WASHER

CONE

BEARINGS

PEDAL BODY

BEARINGS

SEAL

AXLE

1 Some pedals have a cage that you can separate from the pedal body. As it's the cage that makes it awkward to work on pedals, strip it off whenever possible. You may find it easier if you use a vice.

2 The pedal cage sometimes has Phillips screws, or Allen sockets with special heads. Loosen all four a little before you undo them all. Be careful not to distort the cage as you take it off.

3 Dust caps with domed centers are easy to pry out. But sometimes they're flush, and you'll have to use a tiny screwdriver. Dust caps with knurled edges unscrew using pliers with wide-opening jaws.

4 With a separate pedal cage, use a socket wrench or an ordinary box-end wrench to undo the locknut. But on one-piece pedals, only a socket will reach far enough into the cage to loosen the locknut.

5 Once you've loosened the locknut, you can usually undo it the rest of the way with your fingertips. If it won't come off easily, spray the end of the axle with aerosol lube to clean the threads.

6 Take out the lock washer next. Sometimes this is quite difficult as there's a tag that fits into a groove on the axle. Try lifting it up and out with two small screwdrivers, one on each side.

7 The cone is now ready to come out. There may be a screwdriver slot across the face and if so, use that. Or unscrew the cone by sliding a screwdriver between the flats and the pedal center.

8 While you unscrew the cone, hold the axle in the pedal body with your index finger, or you'll get showered with greasy ball bearings. Alternatively, hold it in a vice, perhaps using the wrench flats.

9 Catch all the loose bearings in a cup or on a piece of newspaper. Some won't drop out, so take them out with a pen top or similar item. Clean and inspect all the minor parts, and don't worry if there are minor pits in the bearings.

10 Stick the ball bearings into the inner bearing with grease, then carefully lower the axle in. Holding the axle, turn the pedal up the other way, stick the outer bearings in with grease, and replace cone, washer and locknut.

WHEN YOU NEED TO DO THIS JOB
◆ Before installing new pedals, in case they aren't greased.
◆ If the pedal bearings feel rough and gritty.
◆ When the pedal bearings are loose.

TIME
◆ 20 minutes per pedal, if you have a vice.
◆ 30 minutes per pedal if not.

DIFFICULTY
◆ There are slight difficulties getting to the outer bearing if you can't remove the cage from the body. Otherwise, over-hauling the pedal bearings is very good practice for greasing and adjusting the hub and bottom bracket bearings.

TOOLS
◆ Vice, wide-opening pliers or slip joint pliers.

Toe clips and straps

Riding a bike without toe clips is a bit like riding a horse without a saddle – it can be done, but it's not recommended.

Riders are sometimes put off from using toe clips because they suspect they're unsafe. But experience shows that although it takes a little while getting used to them, they're actually a safety feature. This is because on a bike with toe clips, your foot can never slip off the pedal; as it could do, perhaps, when you make a sudden effort to avoid a car. And even if you do fall off when using toe clips, you instinctively pull your foot out before you hit the ground.

The other advantage of toe clips is that they help you position the ball of your foot over the axle of the pedal. This makes it easier to flex your ankle at the top of the stroke, and directs all the power of your legs into the pedal on the downstroke.

Seldom do you need to actually tighten up the toe straps. Most of the time, the straps just steady the toe clip – you only pull them tight when a major effort is needed, such as going uphill.

When buying toe clips, check that you get the right size for your foot and pedal combination. And when buying pedals, look for proper toe clip holes on the cage, as well as a large tag on the cage to help you pick up the pedal easily with your foot.

1 There are nearly always circular holes in the pedal cage for the toe clip bolts. If not, toe clips are usually supplied with a backing plate to overcome this problem. High-quality pedals often come with special toe clip fittings.

2 Pedals are a good place to mount an extra reflector, as their constant movement makes them even more eye-catching. Where reflectors are mounted on the pedals, move them aside to tighten the toe clip bolts.

5 Pull the toe strap through and position the buckle just outside the pedal cage. Leave enough slack between the buckle and the cage to prevent the metal from cutting through it – this is where a toe strap breaks eventually.

6 With some combinations of toe clips and straps, you can only just squeeze the toe strap through the slots. But if you find it's loose and moves about when you try to tighten it, put a 360° twist in the toe strap to anchor it more firmly.

3 Some road bikes come with platform pedals to save weight. These are made of resin, but alloy versions are also available. Mount the special toe clips using the screws supplied with the pedal. No nuts needed – the holes are threaded.

4 Whether you're using nylon or leather toe straps, feed the strap through the slots cut out of the pedal cage and body. If tight, pull through with pliers. There's usually a special tag to stop the strap from rubbing against the crank.

WHEN YOU NEED TO DO THIS JOB
◆ When equipping a new bike.
◆ Getting the bike ready for winter.

TIME
◆ 15 minutes to install toe clips and straps.
◆ 5 minutes to install reflectors.

DIFFICULTY
◆ No real problems, but you'll sometimes find that the straps are very tight in the slots.

NO SPECIAL TOOLS NEEDED

7 The buckles are not intended to hold the toe strap firmly. Just pass the end under the knurled roller, then through the cut-out in the sprung part. You can now tighten the toe strap, if necessary, by pulling the loose end.

8 It's a particularly good idea to put reflectors on the back of the pedals, where they will be unmissable to over-taking motorists. Most reflectors have a simple two bolt fitting which matches mounting holes on the pedal cage.

Chainrings and cranks

If you're not quite sure which type of crankset and bottom bracket you're dealing with, refer back to the beginning of this chapter.

Alloy cotterless cranksets are used on the vast majority of recent bikes; and in most cases these have separate, replaceable chainrings. This is very handy if wear reaches the point at which new chainrings are needed, or if you find you want to radically change the gearing. However, manufacturers are not always keen on supplying chainrings on their own, especially non-standard sizes, so you may have to ask your dealer to get hold of one from a specialist outlet. Also bear in mind that the bolt holes can be spaced differently by different manufacturers; consequently, you can't always mix and match the various makes of chainrings and cranks.

Normally chainrings can be bolted to the spider in any position. But the oval type that was popular a few years ago, and the recent types where chain, sprockets and chainring all match, must be installed in a set position in relation to the crank. Check for marks on the back of the chainring and spider, and assemble accordingly.

Cottered cranksets used to be found on most budget utility bikes – but even these now come with steel cotterless cranksets. Nevertheless you can still buy new cotter pins if the old ones get damaged. When buying new ones, remember that there are various different types, so take the old cotter pin along to the bike shop as a pattern.

Removing chainrings

1 Nearly all chainrings are bolted to the spider using chrome Allen bolts. Undo the first bolt a half-turn, then the next one a half-turn, until all of them are loose enough to undo by hand. Extend the Allen if necessary.

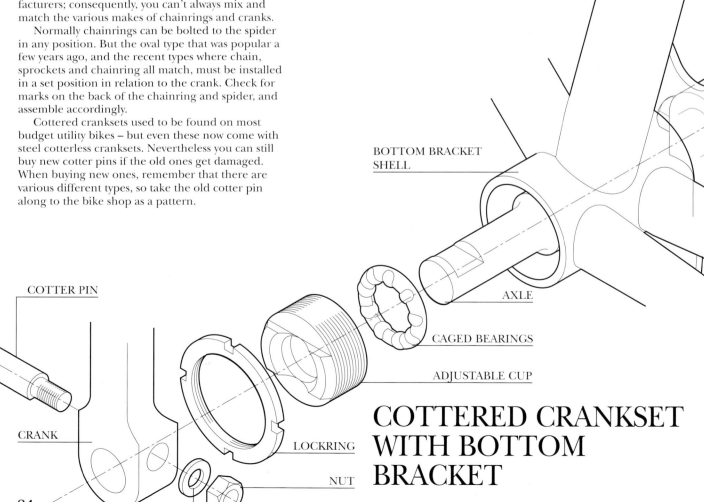

BOTTOM BRACKET SHELL

AXLE

CAGED BEARINGS

ADJUSTABLE CUP

COTTER PIN

CRANK

LOCKRING

NUT

WASHER

COTTERED CRANKSET WITH BOTTOM BRACKET

2 The Allen bolt shown here fits into a sleeve nut that extends through all three chainrings plus the crank spider. Pull off the outer ring by pulling gently on opposite sides – it's a tight fit to prevent unwanted movement.

3 Check for spacers or washers between the chainrings, then lift the outer ring away for cleaning or straightening. The other rings usually remain in place until you draw the sleeve nuts out of the holes in the cranks.

4 In some cases, the small inner ring is bolted in place with a separate ring of bolts. Undo them all, and the inner ring will come off. You may find that the smallest ring is made of steel; this is so that it doesn't wear out.

WHEN YOU NEED TO DO THIS JOB
◆ Chainrings are worn.
◆ Cotter pins work loose.

TIME
◆ 30 minutes for chainrings.
◆ 45 minutes for cotter pins.

DIFFICULTY 🔧🔧🔧🔧
◆ Changing chainrings isn't too bad; cotter pins are trickier.

SPECIAL TOOLS
◆ A bench vice and sharp file make cotter pins easier.

Cottered crankset

1 Undo the bolt and washer on the cotter pin, then give it one sharp blow with a ballpeen hammer. If that doesn't shoot the cotter pin out, find a 1-inch diameter metal bar, place on the pin and hammer on that instead.

2 You can re-use the old cotter pin if it's undamaged; but if you have to put on a new one, use the old one as a pattern. When you're ready to replace the crankset, test-fit the new cotter pin and see whether it goes in far enough.

3 A well-fitted cotter pin has equal length on either side of the crank. Clamp the new pin in a vice, and lightly file the flat. Put it into the crank and see how much farther in it goes, then gauge how much more has to come off.

4 When the cotter pin shows equally on both sides, check that the nut will be under the crank when it points backwards. Lightly hammer the cotter home, then put on the nut. Install the other cotter so that it points the opposite way.

Crank removal

Taking off cotterless cranks can be nerve wracking. But once you've done it a couple of times, you're well on the way to becoming a first-class bike mechanic.

The bottom bracket axle for a cotterless crank is accurately ground into a tapered shape. This spline, and the tapered hole in the crank that fits onto it, are the two most accurately made components on a bike. When installing, reverse the process for removal, but assemble the crank and axle with only the lightest possible coating of grease on the surfaces where they touch. This prevents corrosion between the steel axle and the alloy crank, which makes it easier to get the cranks off later. Some people also like to tap them home lightly with a soft mallet, or else a hammer with a piece of wood as a cushion.

Once installed, tighten the crank bolt up as hard as you can. The extractor tool has a socket wrench for this, but you can usually get more leverage if you use a socket and ratchet handle from a small socket set.

You should also tighten up the bolt every hundred miles or so for the first few hundred miles, as aluminum tends to stretch a little.

Don't ever ride a bike with a loose crank, as the hard steel axle easily damages the soft alloy. And once it's been damaged, it may not be possible to stop a crank from coming loose time and time again. If your cranks won't stay tight, you could try using Loctite stud adhesive on the taper; however, this isn't guaranteed to work. If need be, you may be able to get a spare left-hand crank from your dealer.

1 Cranks should have a dust cover to protect the internal threads. Plastic ones can usually be pried out with a small screwdriver, but top-grade cranksets have alloy or plastic dust caps, screwed in with an Allen key.

WHEN YOU NEED TO DO THIS JOB
◆ For access to the bottom bracket.
◆ When bike needs a very thorough cleaning.

TIME
◆ Allow 30 minutes the first time, so that you can check carefully as you go.
◆ 10 minutes once you're used to the job.

DIFFICULTY ✗✗✗✗
◆ You need a delicate touch when screwing the extractor into the crank, and quite a lot of force when actually pushing the crank off the axle.

TOOLS
◆ Correct crank extractor with undamaged threads. Socket set also useful.

2 Part of the extractor tool is a socket wrench that fits the crank bolt. Check that it's a tight fit on the bolt head. Then use an open-ended wrench to turn it counterclockwise, undoing the bolt. You can also use a normal socket set here.

3 You should be able to undo the crank bolt most of the way with your fingers, then lift it out. Check that you don't leave a large washer behind, as this will prevent the extractor tool from working properly.

4 Prepare to remove the crank by checking that the threads on the extractor tool, and the internal thread that it screws into, are both clean and undamaged. Slowly screw the extractor into the thread.

5 It should screw in easily in about four or five turns. If it tightens up in the first couple of turns, the extractor is probably going in at an angle. You must then take it out, and screw it in absolutely straight.

6 Once it's straight, gently tighten the extractor into the crank with a wrench. Screw the shaft in by hand at first, and then with the aid of a wrench. Brace yourself by holding on to the end of the crank.

7 It takes quite a lot of effort to remove a crank. So if it suddenly gets easier, stop and check everything, as you might be damaging something. Once the crank is off, undo the extractor with a wrench.

8 A few high-end cranksets can be removed by simply unscrewing the central Allen bolt. When re-assembling, use Loctite stud adhesive to ensure that the insert doesn't come loose inside the crank.

Cartridge bottom brackets

The mostly heavily loaded bearing on a bike is the bottom bracket. It's also the most difficult to get at – so anything that cuts down on maintenance is welcome.

Though already found on lots of new bikes, cartridge bottom brackets can also be put on almost any bike with a cotterless crankset, without any modification to the bottom bracket shell in the frame. This is a worthwhile upgrade, because although not quite maintenance free, a cartridge bracket is fitted with effective seals around the axle, which prevent water penetration in most conditions. In addition, a cartridge bracket has better bearings, thereby reducing friction so you go faster for the same amount of effort.

Cartridge brackets are supplied by most crankset manufacturers, but they're also available from independent suppliers, who are normally less expensive; also, the quality is at least as good as original equipment types. The main variable when buying is axle length, so take the old axle along to the shop as a pattern.

The example shown here is the budget Shimano cartridge system, where the retaining ring fits in from the chain side. But other types, including alternative Shimano types, operate the opposite way, with the retaining ring on the non-chain side.

Road riders seldom need to touch a cartridge bottom bracket, and may not find it worth buying the special tools needed to install and remove them. Mountain bikes are more likely to need service.

If you find that the threads in the bottom bracket shell are tight, clean them up with aerosol lube, and by screwing an old bottom bracket cup in and out a few times.

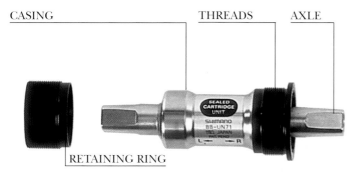

CASING   THREADS   AXLE

RETAINING RING

WHEN YOU NEED TO DO THIS JOB
◆ Upgrading from a standard bottom bracket.
◆ Installing a new crankset.

TIME
◆ 40 minutes – mainly because you have to keep switching from side to side. Also because you may have to clean up the threads.

DIFFICULTY 🔧🔧🔧🔧
◆ Calls for the same combination of delicacy and force as when removing cotterless cranks.

TOOLS
◆ Removal tool, long wrench, old bottom bracket cups.

1 Remove both cranks. Then, for Shimano and some other types, engage the external teeth of the removal tool with the internal teeth of the retaining ring. This tool screws in from the chain side.

4 Now move to the opposite side of the bike, and again insert the removal tool. In this case, you unscrew the cartridge in the normal, counterclockwise direction. This isn't as tricky as removing the retaining ring.

7 Screw the retaining ring in about two-thirds of the way with your fingers only. Don't use the wrench yet, because if the retaining ring won't easily go in part of the way, it'll be very difficult to screw it in all the way later.

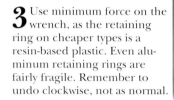

2 With the extractor slotted carefully into the retaining ring, fit a large wrench onto the hexagon and turn clockwise. This undoes the retaining ring that locks the cartridge into the bottom bracket shell.

3 Use minimum force on the wrench, as the retaining ring on cheaper types is a resin-based plastic. Even aluminum retaining rings are fairly fragile. Remember to undo clockwise, not as normal.

5 The cartridge can now be lifted out of the bottom bracket shell. Check that the rubber axle seals, where visible, are in good condition, and that the axle revolves smoothly and easily. Clean the threads.

6 Clean inside of the bracket with a squirt of aerosol lube. Screw retaining ring in counterclockwise with your fingers, from the chain side, to check that the threads are clean. Remove; coat with anti-seize.

8 Switching to the non-chain side of the bike, clean the cartridge and apply anti-seize compound. Screw the cartridge in clockwise as far as you can by hand, checking that the other end of the axle passes right through the retaining ring.

9 Tighten the cartridge into position using the removal tool and wrench. It's fully home when the edge of the threaded portion is flush with the edge of the bottom bracket shell. Remember, this side screws in clockwise.

10 Back on the chain side, tighten the retaining ring counterclockwise until it touches the end of the cartridge, locking it into place. When fully tightened, the retaining ring is almost invisible in the bottom bracket shell.

Cup and axle bottom bracket

One standard bottom bracket may look very different from another. Nonetheless, you can strip them all down in exactly the same way.

Unlike a cartridge bottom bracket, the cup and axle variety demands fairly frequent maintenance. Once a month would not be too often for a bike in heavy off-road use; once a year has to be the absolute minimum for a road bike. But unlike most bike components, where you can easily tell if attention is needed, it's easy to forget the bottom bracket until it has almost seized up.

The main problem with cup and axle bottom brackets is water penetration. When this occurs, the action of the bearings churns the grease and oil into a mixture that does very little to aid lubrication. If you're lucky, the bottom bracket will develop a regular squeak, telling you clearly that something is wrong. By that time, however, the bearing races in the cups will probably be pitted, and some of the hardening will have worn off the axle. This will show up as an area of small pits, where the underlying metal is a different color.

If you suspect any of these problems, install new parts. Luckily there's no problem in fitting a new axle with old cups; or new cups with an old axle; or even mixing different makes of axle and cups. The only point to watch out for is that Italian frames often have a different thread in the bottom bracket shell.

Final adjustment is easier if you install the chainwheel and crank first, and then screw the adjustable cup in or out until you can feel slight movement at the end of the crank. If you tighten the lockring at this point, it will pull the adjustable cup out slightly. This compensates for the way the adjustable cup usually turns slightly when you finally tighten the lockring.

When you strip a bottom bracket, you may find eleven separate bearings, or the bearings may be caged. You can work with either arrangement, but separate ball bearings are probably better because the load is shared between a large number of bearings.

Disassemble and overhaul

1 After removing the cranks, start work on the non-chain side. If the lockring has a series of square cutouts, find a suitable drift pin or cold chisel that roughly fits them. Then, with a ballpeen hammer, tap the lockring counterclockwise.

2 As you tap the lockring, it may drag the adjustable cup with it. After a turn or two, you should be able to unscrew the bearing cup with your fingers. Catch any loose ball bearings as you remove the cup, followed by the axle.

5 When you re-install the bearing cups, you'll be relying on the grease to stop the ball bearings from falling out. Once you've put in all eleven, cover them with more grease. Remove any surplus that spills over into the hole for the axle.

6 Screw the fixed cup into the chain side, tightening it counterclockwise as hard as you can. Steadying it with your finger tips, thread the axle's short side into the adjustable cup, and the long side into the fixed cup already in place.

3 Moving now to the chain side. The main problem is to find an adjustable wrench large enough for the flats on a fixed cup. Once you've found one, undo the fixed cup in a clockwise direction, but be careful not to chip the paint.

4 Clean everything up with solvent and inspect all bearing surfaces. If they're OK, half-fill the cups with water-proof grease and add eleven ball bearings per side. A pen top is ideal for pressing the ball bearings into the grease.

7 Screw in the adjustable cup until you feel it tighten up. Turn the axle. If it feels tight, loosen the adjustable cup until the gravelly feeling goes away. Insert and tighten the lockring, check that the axle turns easily, and re-adjust if needed.

WHEN YOU NEED TO DO THIS JOB
◆ To stop a squeak.
◆ During a full overhaul.
◆ At least once a year.

TIME
◆ Best part of 1 hour.

DIFFICULTY
◆ It's difficult to get the fixed cup in and out if you don't have exactly the right tools. Also, you tend to lose the adjustment when you tighten up the lockring.

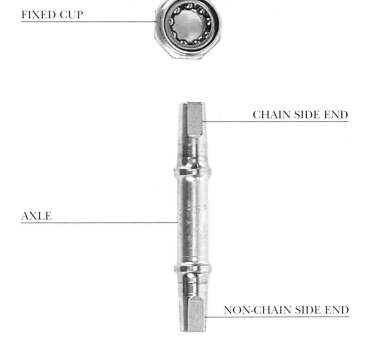

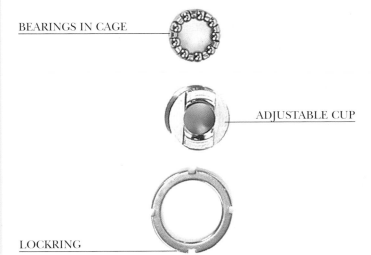

FIXED CUP

CHAIN SIDE END

AXLE

NON-CHAIN SIDE END

BEARINGS IN CAGE

ADJUSTABLE CUP

LOCKRING

91

Cup and axle bottom bracket: 2

Specialized tools make it much easier to overhaul and adjust a cup and axle bottom bracket.

Fixed bottom bracket cups are not easy to work on. Not only do you have to remember that they have a left-hand thread, they are also a tight fit in the frame to ensure that they don't come loose. You can use an adjustable wrench but you're quite likely to chip the paint. A fixed cup spanner will make it easier to fit and remove them but you still have to worry about the spanner slipping off the narrow rim of the cup. So for the ultimate in bottom bracket tools, you'll also need a specialty bottom bracket tool such as Var #30, which holds the spanner onto the fixed cup so it won't slip off.

When you're working on the adjustable bearing cup, a large C-spanner is much less likely to damage the lockring than a hammer and punch.

The adjustable cup often has two holes on the face so that you can screw it in or out with a pin spanner. When a pin spanner is used in conjunction with a C-spanner, you'll find it much easier to hit the point where the axle turns freely, without any play. Just hold the adjustable cup still with the pin spanner while you tighten the lockring. A C-spanner can also be used in conjunction with an open-ended wrench on hexagon bottom bracket.

You should also consider the reasonably-priced sets of pin and lockring spanners. They're small enough to carry on a long trip if necessary.

Using bottom bracket spanners

1 The fixed cup spanner fits right around the outside of the bearing cup. If you push it onto the cup with one hand and turn the spanner with the other, you minimize the chances of it slipping and damaging the paint.

2 When adjusting a standard bracket, use a C-spanner on the lockring. Fit the dog on the spanner into a notch in the lockring and steady your hand on the frame. In this case, you can use an open-ended wrench on the adjusting cup.

Lost bearings

Look out for these basic problems when you're deciding whether to put in new parts. On the left-hand bearing cup above, the chrome has flaked off and the bearing race is covered in tiny pits. The right-hand cup is worn all over and in some areas, the surface of the metal has been worn away. On the axles, the upper one has many small pits while on the lower one, the hardened surface is worn through and the soft metal underneath is crumbling fast.

One piece cranks

This design is only used on kid's bikes but although basically intended to keep down the cost of building small bikes, one piece cranks and the bottom bracket design that goes with them are surprisingly child-resistant. The cranks can get bent in a crash but if you have a big adjustable wrench, you can usually straighten them up without too much difficulty. If the left-hand crank gets badly bent, it's possible to strip down the whole assembly and straighten it up in a vice.

The bottom bracket works well because it's a lot bigger in diameter than a standard one and so contains more ball bearings to share the load. The press-in bearing cups and the axle can get pitted but unless the cups are very badly damaged, maintenance consists of cleaning off all the old grease, regreasing everything and checking that the full number of ball bearings are present.

It's certainly worth going through this overhaul procedure if you've bought a secondhand bike. But judging by the way kids' bikes are sometimes thrown together in the factory, it wouldn't be a bad idea to strip down and grease

1 First thing is to remove the pedals, then undo the lockring in a clockwise direction. It's very thin, so steady the wrench to prevent it from slipping off the flats of the lockring. Once it's free, lift the lockring off the end of the crank.

2 Behind the lockring is a slotted bearing retainer. Position a cold chisel in the slot and tap in a clockwise direction. As you unscrew the retainer, the crank assembly will tilt, so support it with one hand and undo the retainer with the other.

3 Lift the bearing retainer off the end of the crank. If you then tilt the whole assembly until the non-chain side crank is almost horizontal, you can draw it out of the opposite side of the bottom bracket shell. It's steel and therefore heavy.

4 Finally, knock the bearing cups out of the frame. They're a tight fit so when one side of the cup has moved a little, swap the cold chisel to the opposite side and hammer away until it also moves, otherwise they'll jam in place.

the bottom bracket on a brand new bike as well.

It's not always easy to get parts for this kind of chainset or bottom bracket, so wait until you've actually got the spare parts in your hand before you strip the bike down. If your local bicycle dealer can't get

parts, see if you can find a specialist in kids' bikes.

To re-install the bottom bracket, follow the steps given here in reverse but take care to tap the bearing cups back in straight, not at an angle, or you'll never get them in.

WHEN YOU NEED TO DO THIS JOB
◆ You've just bought a new bike and suspect it's not been assembled very carefully.
◆ There's a grinding noise as you turn the cranks.
◆ The cranks have been bent in a crash.

TIME
◆ At least an hour to strip, clean and refit the whole assembly. Longer if you have to straighten out the cranks as well.

DIFFICULTY 🔧🔧🔧🔧
◆ At first it's difficult to see how this assembly fits together. Once you've grasped that, it's also difficult to drive out and refit the bearing cups. The answer is to only drive one side out a little way first. Then go to the opposite side of the bearing cup and drive that out an equal amount and so on.

SPECIAL TOOLS
◆ Large adjustable wrench, ballpeen hammer and cold chisel.

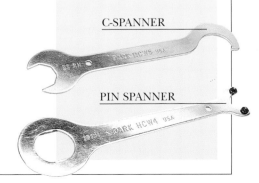

C-SPANNER

PIN SPANNER

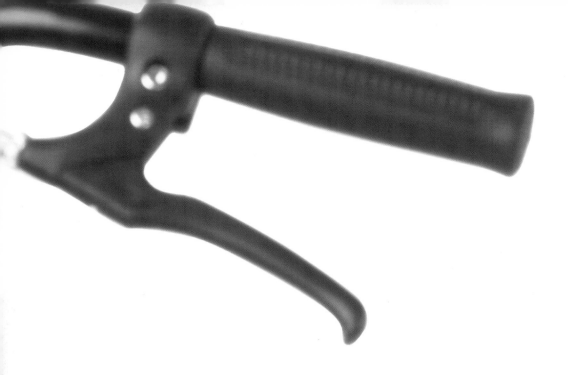

CHAPTER 6

BRAKING SYSTEMS

The brakes are the most safety sensitive area on your bike. So base your working routine on tightening all the nuts and bolts up firmly, checking alignment of the brake pads after every job and then double-checking everything, just in case.

Types of brakes

Nearly all mountain bikes have cantilever brakes. But, although road bikes are equipped with several different designs, none can compare with the cantilever for all-round excellence.

Although very different in design, all the brakes shown on this page work by pressing a brake pad against the braking surface of the wheel rim. Their effectiveness depends on how hard the pad is forced against the rim and how well the pad material bites. This varies with different combinations of materials, as does the rate at which the pad wears. For the best braking performance, always specify the material that the rim is made of when buying new brake pads. Polyurethane pads combine good braking with a low rate of wear, so they're worth the extra cost.

Don't forget that the braking surface of a wheel rim also wears; not as fast as the brake pads, but it can eventually get so bad that the wheel collapses without warning. As a precaution, check the rim when you install new pads and have the wheel rebuilt with a new rim, before the wear gets beyond the stage of shallow grooves in the braking surface.

CANTILEVER BRAKE
Found on nearly all mountain bikes, most hybrids and a few road machines. An excellent design that gives low weight, powerful stopping and lots of clearance for fat tires.

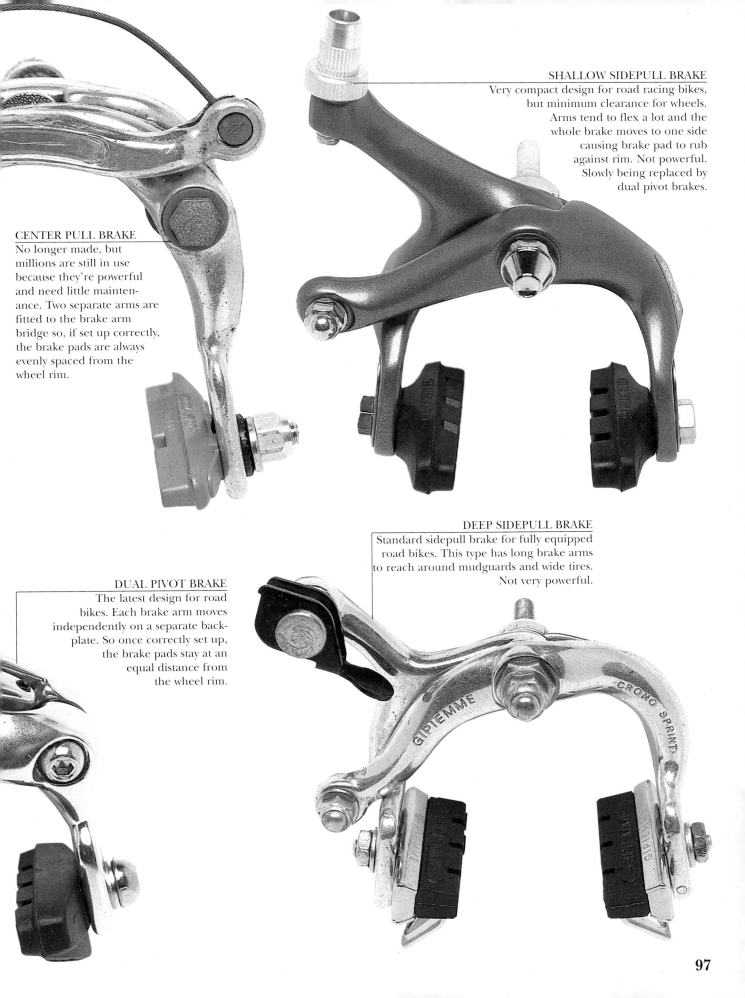

SHALLOW SIDEPULL BRAKE
Very compact design for road racing bikes, but minimum clearance for wheels. Arms tend to flex a lot and the whole brake moves to one side causing brake pad to rub against rim. Not powerful. Slowly being replaced by dual pivot brakes.

CENTER PULL BRAKE
No longer made, but millions are still in use because they're powerful and need little maintenance. Two separate arms are fitted to the brake arm bridge so, if set up correctly, the brake pads are always evenly spaced from the wheel rim.

DEEP SIDEPULL BRAKE
Standard sidepull brake for fully equipped road bikes. This type has long brake arms to reach around mudguards and wide tires. Not very powerful.

DUAL PIVOT BRAKE
The latest design for road bikes. Each brake arm moves independently on a separate backplate. So once correctly set up, the brake pads stay at an equal distance from the wheel rim.

Brake care and inspection

Pad wear causes a gradual fall off in braking performance, so test your brakes frequently in case you don't notice the deterioration.

There is a lot of give in nearly all brake systems. Some of it is cable stretch when you apply a lot of force to the brake lever. The lever itself also flexes a little and so do the brake arms. However, cantilever arms should be quite stiff and if you notice they flex more than a fraction of an inch, consider upgrading.

Road bike brake arms are longer and thinner, so they flex much more than cantilevers. Basic sidepull brakes also move off-center at the drop of a hat, allowing the brake pad to touch the rim. That means the brakes on road bikes tend to need frequent servicing for top braking efficiency.

The combined effect of all this is that if you're not careful, you will run out of brake lever travel in an emergency, before the brakes are fully on. Frequent testing, lubrication and adjustment will guard against this. If you ever notice that the levers are starting to get close to the handlebars in normal use, it's an indication that brake servicing is well overdue.

WHEN YOU NEED TO DO THIS JOB
◆ Whenever you give the chain a thorough cleaning.
◆ If the brake lever seems to have a lot of travel.

TIME
◆ 5 minutes to adjust and lube the brakes.
◆ 5 minutes to tighten the cable.

DIFFICULTY 🔧🔧
◆ Luckily it's very easy to keep your brakes tuned up, so there is no excuse.

NO SPECIAL TOOLS NEEDED

1 Test the brakes by pulling the brake lever. It won't take much effort at first, then the pads will hit the rim and, when you increase the pull, it will just stretch the cable. If the brake lever ends up anywhere near the handlebar, adjustment is needed urgently.

2 On cantilevers, the cable adjuster is on the brake lever. Loosen the thin lock-nut, using pliers if it's stiff, and give the adjuster two turns counterclockwise. Re-test and tighten the cable again, if necessary, until the brake lever feels almost solid.

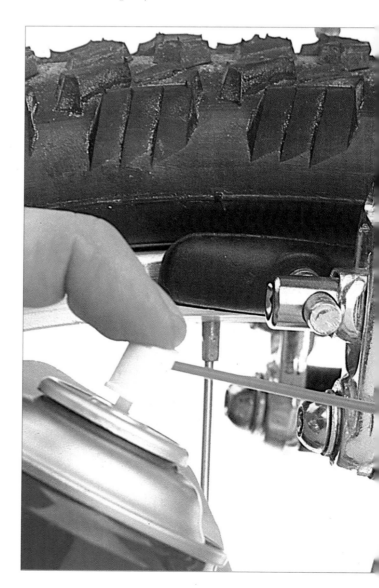

3 The cable adjuster on most road bikes is on the brake arm. Again you loosen the locknut and unscrew the adjuster a couple of turns. The range of adjustment isn't large, so you may have to loosen the anchor bolt, pull the cable through a bit and retighten.

4 Whether or not the brakes need adjusting, you must check the brake pads for wear. But if you've had to tighten the cable up a lot, it's highly likely that the pads are badly worn and need changing. They're completely worn out when the slots are worn away.

5 Give the brake cables a shot of spray lube whenever you lube the chain. However, the brake test should have given you an idea of the pull needed for an emergency stop. If you really have to heave on them and spray lube doesn't have any effect, install a new cable.

6 Brake levers also need lubricating at the same time as the brake cables. Apply spray lube to the pivot, then pull the brake lever hard and squirt lube over the exposed inner cable and nipple, where possible. Road bike levers need exactly the same treatment.

7 The arms of a cantilever brake are bolted on pivots fixed to the frame and this is the only point of friction. Give the brakes a squirt of lube here every time you lube the chain. If the brakes feel heavy and the cables are OK, the pivots could be dirty or corroded, indicating that an overhaul is needed.

8 Sidepull brakes have more internal friction than cantilevers, so give each arm and nut a separate squirt of lube. If the brakes feel heavy, unbolt from the frame and, if a lot of effort is required to squeeze the arms together by hand, disassemble and clean.

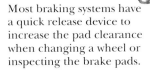

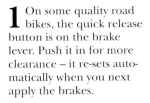

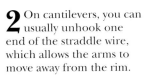

BRAKE RELEASE BUTTON

Quick releases

Most braking systems have a quick release device to increase the pad clearance when changing a wheel or inspecting the brake pads.

1 On some quality road bikes, the quick release button is on the brake lever. Push it in for more clearance – it re-sets automatically when you next apply the brakes.

2 On cantilevers, you can usually unhook one end of the straddle wire, which allows the arms to move away from the rim.

3 Most road bikes have a quick release near the cable adjuster. You pull it upwards when changing the wheel and push it downwards to close the pads up against the rim.

Cantilever brake: disassemble and adjust

The short, stiff arms of a cantilever brake generate plenty of stopping power. You should only have to strip them down when rust or mud gets into the pivots and degrades the performance.

The original type of cantilever brake has a straddle wire that joins the two arms and which is connected to the main brake cable by a metal yoke. This setup works well and is still used by some manufacturers. Recent Shimano cantilevers have a different arrangement. In this, the main brake cable passes through a cable carrier and is connected directly to one of the arms. The other arm is connected to the cable carrier by a link wire.

Link wire types are harder to set up than straddle wire types but give better control over the braking effort. However, when you're working on any type of cantilever brake, it's best to use the adjustment procedure given here together with the advice on installing new cables on the next page.

When you disassemble cantilevers, always inspect the frame pivots as well. If they're rusty, polish with emery cloth and oil, then reassemble with waterproof grease. Check also that the pivots are straight. If they're bent, seek advice from an experienced bike mechanic as it may be necessary to have new pivots brazed on the frame.

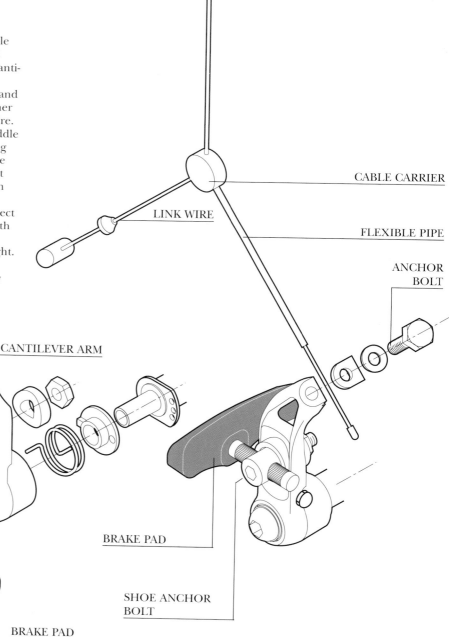

CABLE CARRIER

LINK WIRE

FLEXIBLE PIPE

ANCHOR BOLT

CANTILEVER ARM

BRAKE PAD

SHOE ANCHOR BOLT

BRAKE PAD

1 Screw in the cable adjuster to reduce the tension on the brake cable. If there is a straddle wire, unhook one end and lift it out of the yoke. On a link wire type of brake, undo the anchor bolt with an Allen key and pull the cable out.

2 Now undo the pivot bolt. This frees the cantilever arm, allowing you to slide it off the pivot. Twist it a little if it won't come off easily and try to hold the spring and washer in place on the pivot bolt or they will fly off everywhere.

3 After you clean and grease the pivots, fit the spring into the middle hole on the pivot and screw in the pivot bolt. Turn adjuster with a wrench until each pad is 2 mm (1/16 inch) from rim, lock by tightening the pivot bolt again.

4 Alternatively, there may be a small screw in the side of the cantilever arm that controls pad position. Adjust by turning the screw clockwise to move the pad away from the rim and counterclockwise to bring it closer in.

5 Try to have the pads equally spaced about 2 mm (1/16 inch) from the rim. Sometimes the pads are also toed in about 1 mm (1/32 inch), but this varies with the type of brake and brake pad. This point is covered on page 108.

WHEN YOU NEED TO DO THIS JOB
◆ Brakes feel stiff or jerky when you pull the brake lever.

TIME
◆ 30 minutes.

DIFFICULTY
◆ It's sometimes tricky to put the spring in the hole on the pivot and to adjust pad clearance.

NO SPECIAL TOOLS NEEDED

New cables for cantilevers

Setting up a cantilever brake is a combination of getting the cable length right and adjusting the cantilever arms correctly.

Basic disassembly and adjustment of all cantilever brakes follows the pattern laid out on the previous page. But when installing new cables, it is important to identify the different types, so you use the right procedure.

The commonest type is the straddle wire brake, mostly found on budget bikes. A short straddle wire joins the brake arms and sits in a channel at the back of the metal cable carrier. This cable carrier is connected to the main brake cable by a simple anchor bolt, so it is easy to adjust cable length – the only problem is that you have to guess how long to make the brake cable in the first place and then shorten or lengthen it as required.

On both of the other types, the brake cable is bolted to one of the brake arms, with a short link wire joining the cable carrier to the other brake arm. The early designs have a cable carrier with a bolt running through it, or two separate slots for the cable. The wide slot is used when adjusting the cable, the narrow one the rest of the time.

Recent link wire brakes have a cable carrier with a diagonal line running across it, or a round window for the link wire nipple. The first step when installing a new cable is to slot it in to the cable carrier. Then slide the flexible hose on to the brake cable and fit the cable into the anchor bolt on the brake arm. Set the length of the brake cable so that the flexible hose touches both the cable carrier and the brake arm, then tighten the anchor bolt. Now hook the link wire into the other brake arm and check that the link wire points slightly over the top of the diagonal line, as in the top picture in Step 7.

Next, adjust the spring tension with the small Phillips screws at the back of the brake arms. It is correct when the cable carrier hangs directly below the end of the housing. Now fit the brake pads with 1 mm (1/32 inch) toe-in but don't worry if they touch the rim at this stage.

Lengthen the brake cable so there is a 2 to 3 mm (about 1/8 inch) gap between the end of the flexible hose and the brake arm. When you have done so, the link wire should line up with the diagonal line across the cable carrier, as in the bottom picture on Step 7. Provided it does, center the brake pads using the Phillips screws again. Finally, make sure there is at least 20 mm (3/4 inch) free cable above the cable carrier and set brake pad clearance using the cable adjuster.

WHEN YOU NEED TO DO THIS JOB
◆ Brakes tend to grab or lock the wheel.
◆ Cable is frayed or broken.
◆ Lots of effort needed for emergency stops, suggesting the cable is sticking somewhere.

TIME
◆ 10 minutes to install a new cable in a straddle wire brake.
◆ 20 minutes for a link wire brake.

DIFFICULTY 𝄞𝄞𝄞𝄞
◆ It's easy working on a straddle wire brake, but link wire brakes need careful adjustment to achieve a good balance between stopping power and delicate control.

SPECIAL TOOLS
◆ A fouth-hand tool is useful but not essential.

Link wire cantilevers

1 Screw in the cable adjuster and pull out the old cable. Check that the new nipple fits, grease it lightly and insert the nipple into the hole. Slide the housing over the inner cable and slot both in to the adjuster.

5 Finally, move the brake cable into the narrow slot in the cable carrier. If the pads are not close enough to the rim, bring them in closer with the cable adjuster.

7 The lower picture shows how the link wire lines up with the diagonal line on the cable carrier on new types of link wire brakes when the brake adjustment is complete.

Straddle wire cantilevers

2 On the early type, unhook the link wire from the brake arm next. Then, feed the new brake cable through the wider slot in the cable carrier and slide the flexible hose over the end of the cable.

3 Set the length of the brake cable so that the flexible hose touches both the cable carrier and the brake arm. Hook the link wire back into the other brake arm and adjust the spring tension.

4 With the brake pads equally spaced from the rim, the cable carrier should sit directly below the cable hanger with at least 20 mm (¾ inch) of free cable above it. Adjust the cable if necessary.

1 Feed the brake cable into the anchor bolt on the cable carrier and tighten lightly. Squeeze the brake pads against the rims and see if you can now lift the straddle cable into the channel on the back of the cable carrier. If it's a tight fit, lengthen the main brake cable slightly. If it is too loose, reduce the length of the cable a little. Tighten anchor bolt.

6 On later types of link wire cantilever, the cable fits into the brake lever and the cable carrier in roughly the same way. But once the brake pads are centered, the brake cable length is adjusted to leave a gap of 2 to 3 mm (about ⅛ inch) between the end of the flexible hose and the brake arm.

2 With the brake off, the pads should now sit 2 mm (¹⁄₁₆ inch) from the rim. If necessary, correct the clearance with the cable adjuster. For maximum braking power and control, the straddle wire should roughly form a right angle. If it does not, loosen the anchor bolt on the brake arm and adjust the length of the straddle wire. Finally, check that there is enough free cable above the cable carrier for the brake to come on fully.

Sidepull brake: adjustment

It shouldn't be necessary to strip down and rebuild sidepull brakes very often but if grit gets between the washers and the brake arms, it's the only way to get them working smoothly again.

All the moving parts of a sidepull brake pivot on the central pivot bolt. This creates a lot of friction, although nylon or brass washers are used to minimize it. When you disassemble sidepulls, lay all the parts out in order to help you keep track. If you find any washers are damaged or missing, replace them. They don't have to be an exact fit, so you may be able to use parts from another make or secondhand parts.

If you find your sidepulls tend to stick on, it may be possible to increase the spring pressure by reversing the nylon pad where the spring touches the brake arms. Brake levers are often spring-loaded as well, to make sure that the brakes release as soon as you let go of the brake lever.

You will probably find that your sidepulls constantly move to one side, allowing the brake pad to rub against the rim. If you put a heavy washer on the pivot bolt so it's sandwiched between the brake and the fork, you will find it easier to center the brakes and they will probably stay centered longer.

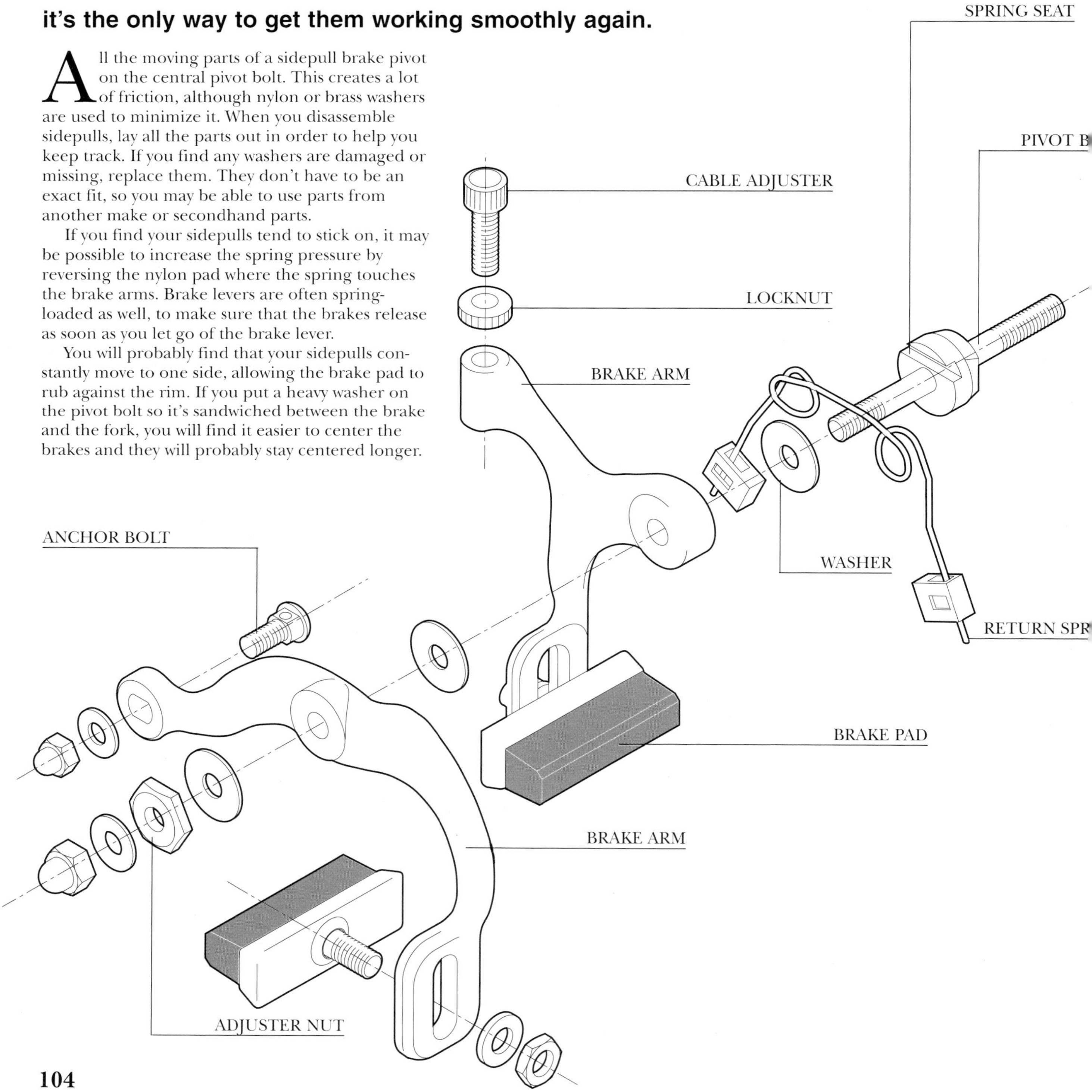

SPRING SEAT

PIVOT B

CABLE ADJUSTER

LOCKNUT

BRAKE ARM

WASHER

RETURN SPR

ANCHOR BOLT

BRAKE PAD

BRAKE ARM

ADJUSTER NUT

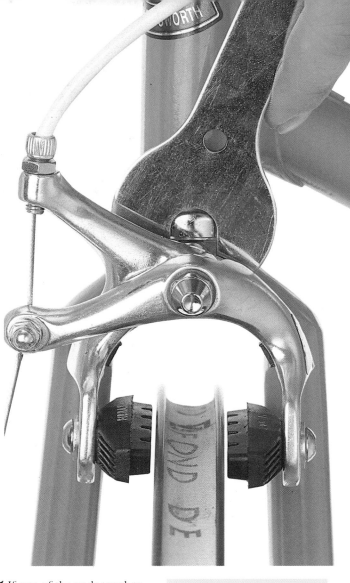

1 Pull off the cable endcap and undo the anchor bolt. Now pull gently on the housing; with luck the inner cable will come out without fraying. Once it's free, the nipple will drop out of the cable anchor in the brake lever.

2 Check how the brake is fixed to the forks next. Sometimes there is a self-locking nut, more likely an Allen-head sleeve bolt. Undo with a wrench or Allen key, but remember, these are not interchangeable.

3 Pull the brake away from the forks and undo the adjuster nut holding everything in place on the pivot bolt. Sometimes this nut is at the front, sometimes the back. Disengage the spring, then pull the brake arms off.

4 Clean and re-assemble, coating all points where friction occurs with anti-seize. Adjust the nuts on the pivot bolt for minimum friction between the arms without excess movement. Bolt back onto the forks and center brake.

5 If one of the pads touches the rim, center the brake next. Loosen the main nut, using a thin wrench to hold the pivot bolt so that the pads are evenly spaced from the rim, then retighten. It will take a couple of tries to get it right.

WHEN YOU NEED TO DO THIS JOB
◆ Installing new cable doesn't lighten brake action.
◆ Braking action feels rough.

TIME
◆ Half an hour to strip, clean and re-assemble each brake. But it can take ages to center them.

DIFFICULTY ⚲⚲⚲⚲
◆ You may find it difficult replacing the spring as it's quite powerful and you will definitely find it difficult to center the brake pads.

NO SPECIAL TOOLS NEEDED

Dual pivot brakes

When fitting a dual pivot brake, check that you've got the brake pads an equal distance from the rims, then tighten the Allen-head bolt. As the brake arms pivot on a separate back plate, the pads should stay centered. If you find that they keep going off center, carefully adjust the Phillips screw on the brake arm.

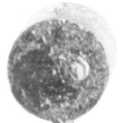

New cables for sidepull brakes

If you install them carefully and keep them lubed, sidepull cables will last for years. But if they're frayed or the brakes tend to stick on, new cables are urgently needed.

Unlike gear cables, brake cables are all more or less of the same quality. The big manufacturers themselves sell prepacked cable sets, but the cables from independent suppliers are of roughly the same quality. Some riders prefer stainless steel cables because they look good and have low friction. Brake cables are thicker than gear cables, so it's important to use sharp cable cutters or you will just crush the cable and it will immediately fray. Once you've cut the cable to length, install a cable endcap to prevent fraying later.

Brake housing is also thicker than the type intended for gears. It can be cut to any length and you use the same type whether it's routed under the handlebar tape, comes out of the top of the brake lever or goes through the frame.

There is no problem mixing different makes of brake lever and brake, so, if you want to swap from old-style levers to the type where the cable goes under the handlebar tape, you only have to buy a pair of new levers.

Rubber hoods around the brake levers make a worthwhile contribution to rider comfort. If you're considering installing a pair, the best time to do it is when you're putting on new brake cables.

1 Frayed cables tend to catch in the anchor bolt as you pull them out, so cut them where convenient and extract the remains with pliers. It will be easier to pull the nipple end out of the brake lever if you slide the housing off first.

6 Spray lube into the cable housing until it bubbles out the other end. Thread the inner cable into the housing. If the cable emerges from the top of the brake lever, the housing sits in a separate ferrule that fits into the lever.

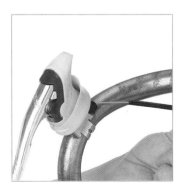

WHEN YOU NEED TO DO THIS JOB
◆ Brake cable is frayed.
◆ Lubing the cable doesn't free it.

TIME
◆ 20 minutes if the cable is routed under the handlebar.
◆ 15 minutes if it sprouts out of the top of the brake lever.

DIFFICULTY ✎✎✎
◆ The only real problem is pulling the new cable tight enough to bring the pads close to the rim. A fourth-hand tool helps here.

TWO NIPPLES, ONE CABLE
Brake cables are sometimes supplied with a different nipple at each end. One is a pear-shaped nipple for the hooded brake levers usually found on drop handlebars. The other is a drum-shaped nipple for various brake levers on flat handlebars. This includes mountain bikes with cantilever brakes and utility bikes with flat touring handlebars and sidepull brakes.

You have to cut one or other of the nipples off before you can use the cable but make sure the cutters are sharp or it will fray immediately.

2 In some cases, you may have to peel back the rubber hood and pry out a plastic cover to get at the nipple. If the cable runs under the handlebar tape, undo that next, because that will make it easier to install the cable later.

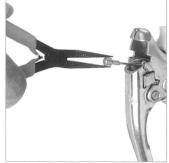

3 Working from the brake end of the housing, try pushing the inner cable out. The nipple should pop out of the brake lever, allowing you to pull the rest out with pliers. If the nipple doesn't move, lever it out with a screwdriver.

4 If the plastic housing is cut or kinked, cut a new length of cable housing and smooth off the cut end if necessary. Use the old housing as a guide to the length of the new one.

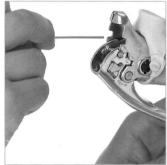

5 In the newer type of brake lever, the inner cable passes through a guide hole at the back, emerging by the inner curve of the handlebars. On the older type of brake lever, the cable simply emerges from the top of the brake lever.

7 Thread the inner cable into the housing and turn the cable anchor until it's in the right position, then slot nipple into place. Seat the cable in the side of the brake lever, then fix it in place with handlebar tape.

8 Once the nipple is in place, keep the inner cable under slight tension to prevent it from slipping out again. Pass it through the cable adjuster, and the anchor bolt, then pull it tight. Check that the nipple is still in the cable anchor.

9 Make sure the adjuster is screwed right in, then find a box-end wrench to fit the anchor bolt. Hold the brake pads with one hand and pull the cable tight with the other. Tighten the anchor bolt and check adjustment.

10 Alternatively, tighten the anchor bolt a little and use a fourth-hand tool to tension the brake cable and pull the brake pads into the rim. Fully tighten the anchor bolt, then use the cable adjuster to fine-tune clearance.

Installing new brake pads

Safety is the main consideration when you're inspecting or installing brake pads. Check wear frequently but, above all, don't ever let the pads touch the tire – they could wear right through and cause a sudden blowout.

Before changing pads, check the condition of the rims, looking first for wear. Light grooves in the braking surface are normal, but if the metal surface seems to have been eroded by the brake pads in any way, have new rims installed without delay. Look also for deposits of pad material and check if the rims feel rubbery or slippery. If there is any sign, try cleaning the braking surface first with alcohol or, if that doesn't work, acetone. Then scour the rims lightly with an abrasive-backed dish pad. This will give the new brake pads a clean rim to bite on.

Most brake pads are molded in one piece with the holder, but always check the instructions to see if toe-in is recommended. In some cases pads are supplied with a special spacer to help set them correctly. By letting the front of the pad touch first, toe-in takes up the natural spring in the brake arms, so preventing chattering when the brakes are applied gently. Check also if there is a particular direction to orient the pads. This is usually indicated by an arrow but in some cases, the slots in the pad are arrow-shaped. Both should be installed so they point in the direction of rotation of the wheel.

Sometimes pads slide into separate holders and are held in place there with a short Phillips screw. To install new pads, undo the screw, push the pad out, press in the new one and re-install. Always check that the closed end of the holder faces forwards. Where the pads are curved, they must be positioned so that the curve of the pad exactly follows the curve of the wheel rim.

Dual pivot and most centerpull brakes are fitted with brake pads the same as sidepulls. But Mafac centerpulls have a multi-adjustable brake pad clamp similar to the one used on cantilevers. When putting a new brake cable on any centerpull brake, use the method given for straddle wire cantilevers.

Cantilevers

1 Loosen the cable adjustment at the lever and then unhook the link or straddle wire from the brake arm. Undo the nut at the back of the shoe anchor bolt, preventing it from moving with an Allen key in the front of the bolt.

Sidepulls

1 Screw the cable adjuster in and operate the quick release so there is some give in the cable, then undo the brake pad. Sometimes it's a bolt, sometimes an Allen bolt. Squeeze the pad out between brake and rim.

SAFETY FIRST

If you don't install brake pads securely, there is a real danger that they will come loose and fall into the spokes, possibly throwing you off your bike. If you position them too high, they will rub through the tire and cause a blowout. Position them too low and they will soon lose their grip.

Re-surfacing worn pads

When brake pads are positioned incorrectly, a ridge of pad material sometimes forms, preventing you from aligning the brake pads correctly with the rim. The cure is simply to cut the ridge off with a sharp utility knife. And if the resulting pad surface is very uneven, flatten it by rubbing the pad surface on a medium grade sandpaper. Don't expect full stopping power until the pads have had a few miles to bed into the rims.

2 Pull the pad holder out of the shoe anchor bolt and check the condition of the pad. If there is a ridge either top or bottom, don't misalign the new pad in the same way. Watch out for a screw holding the pad in the cartridge.

3 If you decide new pads are needed, slip the pad holder into the shoe anchor bolt and allow 1 mm ($\frac{1}{32}$ inch) clearance at the top of the rim. Make sure the pad doesn't overlap the rim at the bottom either.

4 Tighten the shoe anchor bolt securely and check again later. And remember that you may have to position the pad with the arrow on the side facing in the direction of wheel rotation and with the front toed in 1 mm ($\frac{1}{32}$ inch).

WHEN YOU NEED TO DO THIS JOB

◆ Pads are worn past the wear line or the slots have all worn away.

TIME

◆ 20 minutes, including alignment of pads and readjustment of cable.

DIFFICULTY 🔧🔧🔧

◆ Not too difficult, especially on road bikes.

NO SPECIAL TOOLS NEEDED

2 Check the instructions in case there is an arrow on the pad to indicate which way to install it. Slip the pad into the slot and tighten lightly. Do up the quick release and pull the brake lever a few times to normalize everything.

3 Pull the brake lever again and note where the pad hits the rim – don't try to align it in the rest position. Go for clearance at the top of the rim but no overlap at the bottom. Firmly tighten the bolt and road test.

CHATTER AND SQUEAK

If brake pads are installed parallel with the rim or – even worse – toe out, there is often a mysterious chatter or a squeak when the brakes are applied. On sidepulls, this can be cured by taking out the wheels and bending the brake

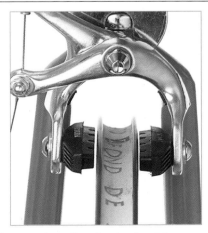

arms with an adjustable wrench so they toe in about 1 mm ($\frac{1}{32}$ inch). Don't suddenly twist the brake arm, apply gentle pressure at first and slowly increase until it bends.

Brake levers

When a brake lever is correctly positioned, you should be able to achieve maximum stopping power, without moving your hands from their normal position on the bars and in full control of the steering.

Mountain bike brake levers all follow roughly the same design. The main difference between budget and quality levers is the provision of reach adjustment and the quality of materials. Don't forget about reach adjustment, as a comfortable hand position on the brake lever helps to prevent you from locking up the brakes on the loose. It's particularly valuable for short riders.

Utility road bikes also use the flat style of brake lever with both sidepulls and cantilevers. They don't really have enough travel or leverage for sidepulls, so make sure you keep the brakes well maintained if your bike has this type of setup.

Racing bike brake levers are all very similar, unless you have STI or Ergopower. On these, the gear change mechanism fills the hood, so the Allenhead bolt is to one side, visible only when you peel back the outside edge of the rubber hood.

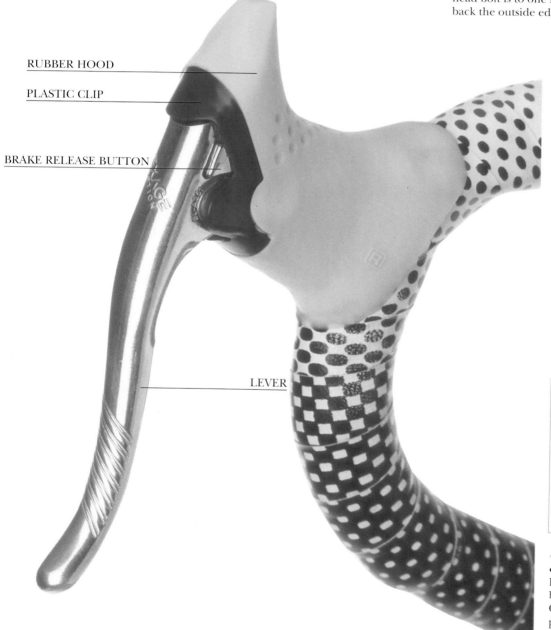

RUBBER HOOD

PLASTIC CLIP

BRAKE RELEASE BUTTON

LEVER

Road bikes

1 To reduce the effort needed for braking, lube the brake lever pivot in case it's sticky with old oil. Pull the brake lever next, so you can spray lube on the end of the cable – then work the lever so the lube spreads along it.

3 To remove the brake lever without undoing the handlebar tape, loosen clamp bolt and pull off handlebar. On STI gear and brake levers, pull the edge of the rubber hood back and undo the bolt with an Allen key.

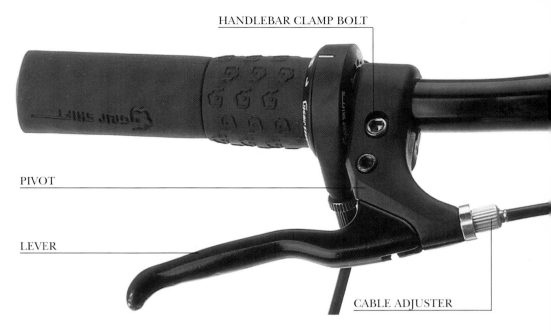

HANDLEBAR CLAMP BOLT

PIVOT

LEVER

CABLE ADJUSTER

Mountain bikes

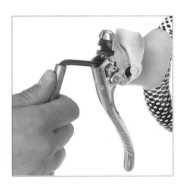

2 If the brake lever is loose or you want to adjust its position, remove cable and, at the back of the hood, you will see the clamp bolt. You may be able to use a screwdriver, but if you have to use an Allen key, go for extra leverage.

COMBINED BRAKE LEVERS AND SHIFTERS ON MTBS
To remove the shifter, take off both cable adjusters and undo the small Phillips screws that hold the indicator in place. Pull off and then undo the Allen bolt holding the shifter to the brake lever. To re-install, select bottom gear on shifter and line up the needle with the vertical line on the body, then insert the Allen bolt.

1 Mountain bike and hybrid brake levers are exposed to the wet, so lube the pivots frequently. Pull the brake lever so that you can lube the cable as well. Give the cable adjuster a squirt of lube so it doesn't stick or corrode.

2 To adjust position or take off the brake lever, loosen clamp bolt. Where the gear shifter is fitted to the brake lever, the clamp bolt is usually tucked under the shifter lever. Push it fully forward to get at the clamp bolt.

WHEN YOU NEED TO DO THIS JOB
◆ Brakes feel heavy but not gritty, so the cables need lubricating.
◆ The position of your hands when applying the brakes or resting on the brake levers is uncomfortable, so you need to alter it or adjust the distance your hands have to stretch to the brake lever or both.
◆ You're installing new handlebars.

TIME
◆ 2 minutes to lube the levers and cables.
◆ 5 minutes to tighten loose brake levers.

◆ 15 minutes to remove both brake levers.

DIFFICULTY 🔧🔧🔧
◆ With racing bike brake levers, it is sometimes difficult to reach the clamp bolt at the back of the lever or remount the brake lever to the handlebar clamp on the handlebars.

SPECIAL TOOLS
◆ Long workshop Allen keys or, better still, T-shaped Allen keys are extremely useful when working on road bike brake levers.

3 On the better MTB brake levers, there is a small Phillips screw just behind the cable adjuster. This allows you to alter the reach. Try to adjust it so that you can do an emergency stop using your middle three fingers only.

CHAPTER 7

WHEELS & TIRES

Despite their light weight, bike wheels usually come unscathed through potholes, punctures and pile-ups. Nevertheless, they are the most important component on any bike, so buy the best tires and wheels you can afford.

Wheel care and inspection

Sooner or later, you'll have to walk home with a punctured tire or a buckled wheel but if you use the routine laid down here, it shouldn't happen very often.

Whether you ride on tough mountain bike 'knobbies' or lean-as-a-greyhound road bike wheels, they need very much the same sort of care. Even on budget bikes, the wheels should rotate pretty smoothly. On quality bikes, they should run as smooth as silk. If they don't, strip and clean them immediately or you may permanently damage the bearings. Nearly all hubs are now fitted with a seal to keep the water out, so once you've got them running right, they should be OK for quite a while.

The only regular maintenance hubs need is a few drops of heavy oil. Some have an oil port in the barrel where you can squirt the oil in but most do not. But even if the hubs are sealed, you can always apply some oil around the cones and it will eventually work its way through the seals and into the hub. Take care to clean the cone area thoroughly first, otherwise the oil will carry dirt into the bearings.

Punctures are a big problem but most happen because tires aren't pumped up hard enough, they're worn out or a stone has been allowed to work its way through into the tube. It follows that you can prevent most punctures with a little timely maintenance.

QUICK
RELEASE
LEVER

VALVE

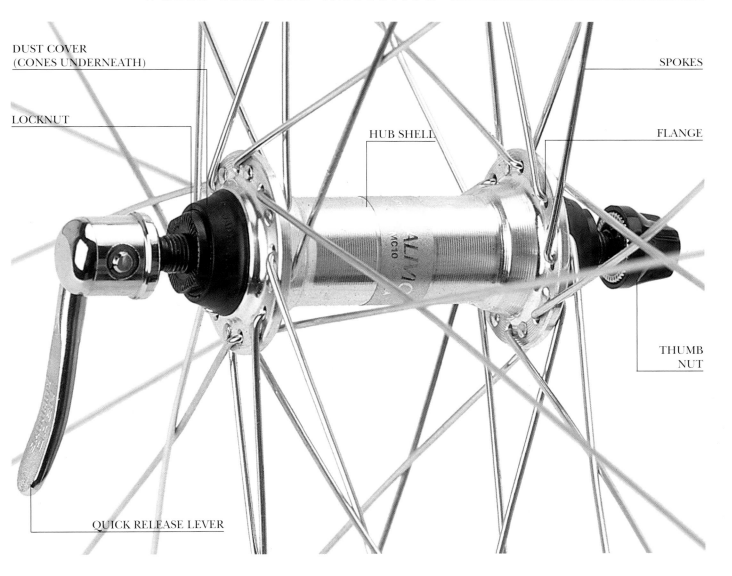

DUST COVER
(CONES UNDERNEATH)

SPOKES

LOCKNUT

HUB SHELL

FLANGE

THUMB
NUT

QUICK RELEASE LEVER

1 Lift the front wheel off the ground and try to move the rim from side to side. Any movement here suggests that the bearings need adjusting. Next, rotate the wheel slowly with one hand. If you can feel or hear any traces of grittiness in the bearing, the hub needs stripping down and greasing.

2 Even if there is apparently nothing wrong with the hub bearings, you should give them a few drops of heavy oil occasionally. If there is no oil port, cover one side of the hub with spray lube to clean it, then lay it flat and squeeze some heavy oil around the edge of the bearing cone.

3 Examine the tire for cuts, stones buried in the tread and sidewall damage. Then spin the wheel slowly to check for bulges in the tire walls. Check if the rim is straight and true at the same time. Replace damaged tires and dig any stones out of the tread with a small screwdriver.

WHEN YOU NEED TO DO THIS JOB
◆ After every serious ride off-road.
◆ Every couple of months on a road bike.
◆ If you ride through a patch of fresh asphalt.

TIME
◆ Takes 5 minutes as part of a general inspection.

DIFFICULTY
◆ Be vigilant on tires.

NO SPECIAL TOOLS NEEDED

Removing wheels

It sounds easy enough to undo the wheels and pull them out but it's the kind of job where you really need three hands.

When removing or replacing wheels, the first thing to do is operate the quick release on the brakes so there is room for the tire to fit between the brake pads. This is particularly important on mountain bikes. If you've got a workstand, you can remove the wheels with the bike the normal way up. If not, or you're fixing it by the roadside, turn the bike upside down.

Quick release hubs are easy to work with but if you don't do them up tight enough, they can come loose and cause an accident. You'll develop an instinct about how hard you have to push the quick release lever to lock it but if it leaves a mark on your palm when you close it, it's tight enough.

Use three fingers on the wrench when you're tightening up wheel nuts and apply a considerable but not a huge amount of force. The problem when replacing a wheel with axle nuts is keeping it centered between the chain stays while tightening the nuts at the same time. Try to steady the axle with one hand and hold the wrench in the other, then switch.

There is only one position in which you can mount a front wheel. Rear wheels can be mounted anywhere in the dropout but quality frames have built-in guides.

WHEN YOU NEED TO DO THIS JOB
◆ Tire has punctured.
◆ Hub bearings need maintenance.
◆ Back wheel has pulled over to one side.

TIME
◆ 10 seconds to remove and replace front wheel.
◆ 20 seconds to remove back wheel.
◆ 30 seconds to replace back wheel.

DIFFICULTY ✗✗✗
◆ There is a bit of a knack getting the chain on the sprockets and getting it past the rear derailleur.
◆ You've also got to learn how to do up the back wheel nuts in turn, a little at a time, keeping the wheel centered while you do so.

NO SPECIAL TOOLS NEEDED

SAFETY SYSTEMS
Watch out for the safety system on some bikes with wheel nuts. It consists of an oval washer that fits in between the wheel nut and the fork. The tab on the washer has to be fitted into a slot

on the fork end, before you fit the wheel nut. Once the washer is in place, the wheel nut is tightened in the normal way and the wheel can't fall out.

Bolt-in wheels

1 First, undo both wheel nuts three or four turns. Proper wheel nuts have a built-in toothed washer to grip the frame – change to this type if your bike only has plain wheel nuts with a separate washer.

2 Pull the rear derailleur backwards so that the chain cage pivots right out of the way. That will allow the wheel to slide forward out of the dropouts, though it will be tight. Give it a hefty push with your free hand if it sticks.

3 As the wheel drops out of the frame, it will bring the chain with it. So let the rear derailleur return to its normal position and try to lift the wheel away. If it won't come, you'll have to lift the chain with your fingers or a tool.

4 To replace the wheel, pivot the rear derailleur backwards again and engage the top sprocket with the top run of the chain. Lift the wheel so that the sprockets pass over the rear derailleur, bringing the chain with them.

5 Check to see if the rim is centered and lift the axle into the frame. Pull the wheel back to the middle of the dropout, clear of the rear derailleur, finger tighten the nuts. Check that the rim is centered before tightening nuts.

Quick release wheels

1 Loosening a quick release is a finger and thumb operation. Just hook your thumb around the lever and pull hard. As soon as you have overcome the initial locking action, the lever will swing back the rest of the way quite freely.

2 The wheel should fall out as soon as the quick release is operated. But if it's not a perfect fit in the forks, you may have to hold the thumb nut with one hand and give the lever a couple of turns with the other to release it.

3 When replacing the wheel, you may find that you have to spread the forks a little to fit the axle between them. If necessary, you must tighten up the thumb nut so that the quick release almost bites, before you operate the lever.

4 The initial movement of the quick release lever requires very little pressure. By the time it passes halfway, it should need noticeably more force and the final locking stage should take quite a lot. If it doesn't, it's not tight. enough.

RUBBER RIM TAPE

Tires and tubes

Whether you're fixing a puncture, changing the tire or replacing a broken spoke, taking the tube out is always the first step.

Punctures are not always an affliction sent to punish wicked cyclists, but sometimes they can be! If you get a flat and it has not been caused by a deep pothole or a carelessly dropped nail, you've probably been neglecting your tires.

It could be that you're riding with the tires half flat. When you do that, the tires flex a lot as you ride along and the tire walls suffer in particular: they're the most vulnerable part of a tire. A soft tire is also an easy target for a stone or a piece of glass which would simply bounce off a hard one. Finally, when a tire is soft, there is a danger of the tube getting pinched by the rim when going over a bump that a fully inflated tire would take in its stride. If you pump up your tires a little every two or three weeks, you'll eliminate a lot of punctures.

Worn tires could be the other main cause of punctures. Obviously tires wear out with use but the rubber tread also deteriorates over a period of time, particularly if a bike has been left standing on flat tires. Putting on new tires every two or three years will cut out a lot more flats.

Tires reinforced with Kevlar have a built-in resistance to punctures. Kevlar is a strong composite fiber that is woven into a tape and placed under the tread. It takes a very determined nail or stone to penetrate it. Reinforced tires cost about 50 percent more but they do have a longer life.

If you ever get a puncture on the inside edge of the tube, the rim tape is probably damaged or missing altogether, allowing the spoke heads to damage the tube. So check the rim tape every time you take off a tire and fit a new one when it starts to fray around the valve hole. Mystery punctures are sometimes caused by leaking valves. Most bikes are equipped with the Presta type which have a threaded sleeve at the top. Dip the valve in a cup of water and check for bubbles if you suspect a leak.

Removing the tube

1 The location of a puncture is usually obvious but if not, pump up the tire and listen for a hiss. If you can't find the hole, take the tube out, inflate it a little and hold it under water. A stream of bubbles will show where the puncture is.

2 In most cases, you'll easily spot the stone or nail that has caused the flat. If you've just hit a big bump and the tire has gone down fast, the tube may have been pinched by the wheel rim, without any visible damage.

3 If there is a lockring holding the valve in the rim, remove it now. Next, open the valve and bounce the wheel a few times to force out the last of the air. Then go around the wheel, forcing the tire away from the rim in case it's stuck.

4 Go around again, this time pushing both tire walls into the center of the rim. This will make it easier to slip the first tire lever under the tire bead and lever it upwards until the tire wall suddenly jumps right over the wheel rim.

5 Hook the end of the first tire lever on a spoke. Now move six inches around the rim, press the tire back with your thumb and slip the tire lever under the bead again. Lever it up and over the rim. It'll take more effort this time.

6 Repeat with the third tire lever – the middle one will then drop out. Pick it up, move along another six inches and lever the bead up and over the rim again. You should then be able to pull the rest of the bead over the rim with your hand.

7 To get a grip on the tube, reach inside the tire and feel for it with your fingers. Pull the tube out now, right around to the valve. The tire should now be very loose on the rim so lift the bead back and push the valve out.

WHEN YOU NEED TO DO THIS JOB
◆ Fixing a puncture.
◆ Getting ready to install a new tire.
◆ If a spoke needs replacing.

TIME
◆ Take it slowly the first time you do this job – say 10 minutes. But you'll get it down to 3 minutes with a bit of practice.

DIFFICULTY
◆ You always have to be careful not to damage the tube when using tire levers. The other thing you have to get used to is persuading the tire beads to drop down into the well of the wheel rim.

SPECIAL TOOLS
◆ A valve tool is needed to remove the core from a Schrader valve. You can sometimes use an old valve cap to do this – likely to be obtainable from an auto accessory shop.

Woods valves

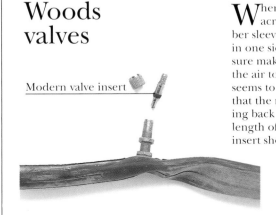

Modern valve insert

When working with old bikes, you may come across the Woods tire valve. These have a rubber sleeve which fits tightly around a tube with a hole in one side. When you pump the tire up, the air pressure makes the rubber balloon out slightly, allowing the air to enter the tube. If a bike with these valves seems to have a mystery puncture, the chances are that the rubber sleeve has perished and air is escaping back through the valve. Install either a new length of valve rubber or the more reliable modern insert shown here.

Puncture repairs

Always use feather edge patches if possible, especially with light tires. They're more reliable and blend into the tube without causing bulges.

Always check the inside of the tire for small stones while it's off the rim, just in case one has worked its way right through the tough canvas of the tire. Then check the tread and sidewalls for cuts and any canvas showing through the outer layers of the tire.

Repair kits usually contain a piece of tire that can be stuck on the inside of the tire to repair minor damage. If the hole is too big for this treatment, you may be able to make a temporary fix by cannibalizing an old tire. Just cut a piece out of the tread and fit it inside the damaged tire. When you

Repairing punctures

1 Even if it's easy to spot the puncture, it's even easier to lose track of it once you've pulled the tube out. So mark the spot with the yellow crayon you'll find in most puncture kits. Don't overdo it.

2 Next, roughen up the area around the puncture with sandpaper, again supplied in most puncture kits. You don't have to scratch the surface, just clean off any dirt or old rubber cement on the surface.

3 When you're satisfied that the tube is clean and dry, select a suitable patch. Apply a thin, even coat of rubber cement around the puncture, then put the tube somewhere out of the wind to dry.

4 If you're using standard rubber patches, wait until the rubber cement is dry. Then lift a corner of the white backing with your fingernail, pull the rest off and press the patch into position.

Replacing tire and tube

3 Make sure the tube is sitting inside the rim and settle the tire on the rim evenly all the way around. Starting at the valve, push the tire over the edge of the rim with your thumbs.

1 Position the valve hole in the rim at the top of the wheel and lift the tire wall so that you can thread the valve in to the rim. Don't screw on the retaining ring yet but do keep the valve upright.

2 Work your way around the wheel, tucking the tube into the deepest part of the rim. Try to avoid twisting or creasing it as you do so. This may be easier if you pump the tube up a little.

pump it up, there'll be a bump in the tread but at least you'll still be moving.

Most cyclists on a long run or a serious off-road ride carry a spare tube and you can also carry a folding tire. On these, the beads are usually made of Kevlar and the tires will usually fit in a bottle cage or under the saddle.

Riders sometimes have trouble pumping up a tire using a push-on adaptor. The main thing is to loosen the valve sleeve nut quite a bit first, and then steady the adaptor by wrapping your index finger around the valve.

WHEN YOU NEED TO DO THIS JOB
◆ To fix a puncture.
◆ When you're installing a new tire.
◆ If one of the spokes needs replacing.

TIME
◆ 5 minutes to repair a puncture, once you've found it.

DIFFICULTY 🔧🔧🔧
◆ Follow each step very carefully. Don't allow dust to settle on the freshly applied rubber cement.

SPECIAL TOOLS
◆ Repare kit, tire levers.

5 Try to position the center of the patch right on top of the puncture and smooth it out from there to avoid trapping any air. Then use the end of a tire lever to press the patch down, especially the edges.

6 With feather edge patches, you also wait for the rubber cement to dry. Pull off the silver foil backing next, position the patch on top of the puncture and press down from the center with a tire lever.

7 After 20 seconds, fold the patch in half. The cover should then split, allowing you to peel it off from the center. Feather edge patches blend into the tube and the edges shouldn't lift at all.

BUMPY RIDE
When a tire is getting really old or it's taking a beating from potholes or bumps, the casing will start to bulge in various places, indicating that puncture resistance is very low. In extreme cases, if you touch down on the damaged area again, the tire will burst and probably wreck the wheel as well. Check your tires and replace them if there are signs of wear.

4 Continue this process all around the tire, pulling the back of the tire in with your fingers and forcing the tire wall over the rim with your thumbs. Try to avoid using the tire levers at all.

5 If you use a tire lever, don't trap the tube against the rim or you'll puncture the tube again. Pump the wheel up a little to straighten out the tube, check that the valve is upright and screw on the retainer.

Strip down hubs

Don't take it for granted that the hub bearings are fine, just because there seem to be no obvious problems. Occasionally check the bearings over and disassemble and re-grease the moment they start to feel a bit rough.

You've probably decided to strip the hubs down because of problems revealed by an occasional inspection. It's OK to leave it at that on road bikes mainly used in dry weather. But if you've been out in a downpour, especially off-road, it's a good idea to check the hub bearings in the next few days. Regular off-road riders should reckon on a routine overhaul every couple of months but road riders can stretch that to a couple of years if the wheels keep on running smoothly.

Most hubs have some sort of rubber seal to keep out the wet stuff but it only works up to a point. So don't ever point a hose at the hubs, let alone a pressure washer, no matter how dirty your bike.

Some seals are external to the hub and fit around the axle, locknut and cone, pressing on the flange of the hub. More often, the seal is set in the flange itself and presses on the outside edge of the cone. In this case, it may be necessary to carefully pry the seal out in order to get at the ball bearings. This second type can be backed up with additional seals made by various accessory manufacturers. They're designed for mountain bikes but there is no reason why they can't be used on other types.

A front hub is shown in the illustrations to keep things simple but you disassemble rear hubs in more or less the same way.

1 Remove the quick release by holding the thumb nut and twisting the quick release lever until it comes to the end of the thread. Watch for the conical springs on either side of the hub.

5 When you've removed the cone and locknut on one side of the axle, you can pull the axle out the other side. Be careful as some of the ball bearings might come with it and fall on the floor.

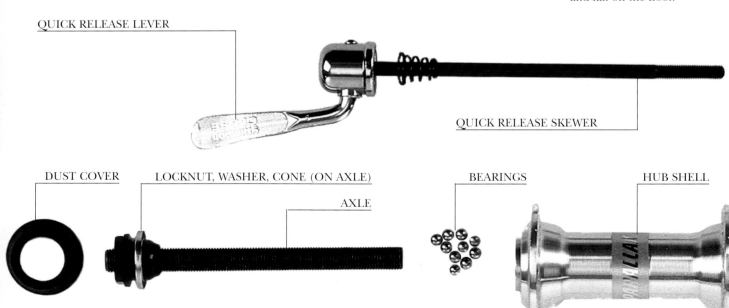

QUICK RELEASE LEVER

QUICK RELEASE SKEWER

DUST COVER

LOCKNUT, WASHER, CONE (ON AXLE)

AXLE

BEARINGS

HUB SHELL

2 On mountain bikes, you'll sometimes find a separate rubber seal which is intended to prevent water from entering the hub bearings – they just pull off. But internal seals are more common.

3 Use a cone wrench to hold the axle still while you undo one of the locknuts. It'll take quite a heave to start with. If you're working on a back wheel, it's usually best to work on the non–chain side.

4 Undo the locknut and pull off the lock washer. This sometimes has a tag which fits into a groove in the axle, so you may have to pry it off with a screwdriver. Finally, undo the cone itself.

6 Almost certainly some ball bearings will be left in the hub, stuck there in the grease. Drag them out with a small screwdriver or a pen top and scrape out as much of the old grease as you can.

WHEN YOU NEED TO DO THIS JOB

◆ When you can't get the hub bearings to run smoothly by adjusting the cones.

◆ During a big overhaul.

TIME

◆ 5 minutes to remove the axle.

DIFFICULTY

◆ This is the easy part, provided that you've got a thin wrench that fits.

SPECIAL TOOLS

◆ At least one cone wrench.

CONE

LOCKNUT

LOCK WASHER

SPRING   THUMB NUT

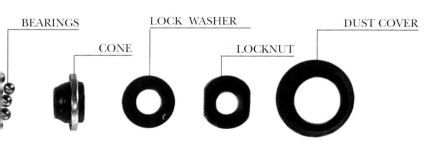

BEARINGS   LOCK WASHER   DUST COVER

CONE   LOCKNUT

Grease and adjust hubs

If hubs need cleaning and fresh grease, go through all the steps here. If they run smoothly but the bearings are loose, go through the adjustment procedure only.

The first thing to do after stripping the hubs down is check the cones for damage. If there is any problem at all, it's best to install new ones. Check also that the axle is straight — if the axle ends appear to move up and down when you turn it, install a new axle too. Most cones have the same thread and shape, so there is usually no problem finding new ones but if you're dealing with budget hubs, it may be simplest to buy a complete new axle.

The core part of this job is adjusting the cones so that they apply the right amount of pressure to the bearings. Aim for the point where you can't feel any movement at all on the axle, and yet the axle turns without any feeling of friction or grittiness.

Finding this exact point is mostly a process of trial and error and even professionals don't expect to hit it first time, every time. So don't worry if you also have to re-adjust the cones a few times.

The problem is that when you tighten the locknut, it increases the pressure on the cones and through them on the bearings. So to get the cone adjustment right, you have to leave just enough slack to make up for the tightening of the locknut.

When you think you've got the adjustment right and the axle turns really smoothly, pop the wheel back into the bike and see if you can detect any movement at the wheel rim. The distance of the rim from the hub magnifies this, so it's OK if you can detect just a tiny amount of movement. Re-check the adjustment after your next ride.

They're the pits

Once you've stripped the hub bearings down, the next step is to inspect the inner surface of the cones for damage and wear. The cone above left is a brand new, high quality item which is the ideal. The middle one is pitted and should not be re-used at any price. The right-hand cone has some wear which will probably accelerate from now on. But it could be re-used if things are desperate.

1 Having cleaned away all traces of old lubricant, coat both bearing races with a thin layer of waterproof grease. Don't be tempted to fill the barrel of the hub with grease or it'll be forced out later and make a horrible mess.

4 If you're re-using old cones, fit one of the them onto the axle and screw it down until there is just a little play left on the bearings. Spin the wheel slowly now — it should already turn much more smoothly than it did before.

5 If you're installing new cones, adjust their position so that the axle is central in the hub. Insert lock washers and locknuts finger tight against the cones. Don't leave out the washers or it'll be hard to adjust the cones.

2 Now fill the bearing races with new ball bearings. They have to be pushed down into the grease to make them stick and to ensure that you put in the correct number. A pen top is ideal for this purpose but you can use your fingers.

3 Now spread a little more grease on top of the bearings. If the old cones are OK, there is no need to undo the one still in place on the axle. But you must clean everything up carefully before inserting it in the hub.

WHEN YOU NEED TO DO THIS JOB
◆ During an inspection, you've found that the hub bearings are not very smooth.
◆ As part of a major overhaul.

TIME
◆ 40 minutes including stripping down and de-greasing.

DIFFICULTY
◆ Provided you've got proper cone wrenches the only real problem is adjusting the cones just right. Don't forget that the grease is quite thick to start with, so the bearings will loosen up a bit later.

SPECIAL TOOLS
◆ You really need two cone wrenches. These are thin wrenches that slip between the cones and the locknuts. But remember, if you abuse them, the jaws will distort and cause problems.

6 If you're re-using old cones, the axle should already be centered and the locknut fully tightened on one side. But when installing new cones, check the axle position and then tighten the locknut up against the cone on one side.

7 Turning to the other cone, screw it in or out until there is a tiny amount of play left, then tighten the locknut against the cone. This final tightening will probably be enough to eliminate that little bit of movement.

Wheel truing and spoke replacement

Don't be afraid to tweak the spokes a little if your wheels are out of true but remember, this is really a job for a professional.

If necessary, your local bike shop will sell you a replacement wheel. You have a choice of standard machine-built wheels or hand-built. If you decide on a hand-built wheel, the weight and strength of the rim, the strength and number of spokes and the quality of the hubs can all be tailored to suit your style of cycling.

The spokes are held into the wheel by square-sided nipples which are tightened or loosened with a spoke wrench. However, the square end is tiny so it's vital to use a tightly fitting spoke wrench. If you don't, you'll round off all the nipples and the wheel will have to be rebuilt.

Occasionally you'll find that the nipples have seized onto the spokes and won't move in either direction. If they won't loosen with spray lube,

again the wheel will have to be rebuilt.

Any time that you tighten a nipple, the end of the spoke pokes a little farther and could puncture the tube. Ideally you should always remove the tire when working on a wheel so that you can file the spoke end flush with the nipple.

When replacing spokes, the crucial thing is to follow the pattern exactly, crossing the same number of spokes and alternating sides where they fit into the hub. Truing a wheel is a matter of increasing the spoke tension on one side to pull the rim straight and slackening it on the opposite side to make up for this. Treat each bend separately and work from the edges to the middle, increasing tension at the edges by a quarter-turn at a time and a half-turn in the middle.

Installing a new spoke

1 Spokes usually break just below the nipple or near the bend close to the hub. It's normally easy to extract the remains but if the spoke has broken on the chain side of the back wheel, you'll probably have to remove the cluster.

2 Thread the new spoke into the empty spoke hole and wiggle it around so that the head seats nicely. Look at the next-spoke-but-one to see if the new spoke goes over or under the spoke that it crosses and follow this pattern.

Truing a lightly buckled wheel

1 Unless you're doing a road-side repair, it's best to take off the tire and tube first. Then fit the wheel in the frame and spin it slowly, noting where and how bad the bends are.

2 If the rim bends to the left, loosen the left-hand spokes a little and tighten the opposite, right-hand ones. Work from the ends of the bend towards the middle. True each bend before moving on.

3 Don't try to do it in one go but work progressively, checking it by spinning the wheel frequently. When the wheel is true, stress relieve the spokes – squeeze parallel pairs – to settle them in place.

The truth machine

It's OK to tighten up a loose spoke or iron out a slight bend in the rim for yourself. However, all the spokes in a wheel should be kept at a high but even tension and once you've loosened some and tightened up others, you may have weakened the wheel considerably. The answer is to let a bike mechanic true up your wheels as soon as they start leaving the straight and narrow. Professionals use a special jig which allows them to correct side-to-side and also up-and-down bends. They also re-tension the spokes so that the wheel stays true for longer.

WHEN YOU NEED TO DO THIS JOB:
◆ As a roadside repair.
◆ When the wheel wanders a bit but you haven't got time to take it to a bike shop.

TIME:
◆ 20 minutes to true a slightly wavy wheel.
◆ 30 minutes to remove a tire and install a new spoke.

DIFFICULTY:
◆ Quite difficult because you have to balance loosening and tightening spokes. Take it slowly and check frequently that you're improving things, not making them worse.

SPECIAL TOOLS
◆ Spoke wrench to fit your wheel. The commonest spoke sizes are 14, 15 and 16 but check before you buy. Don't buy a combination spoke wrench because they're difficult to use and very likely might damage the nipples.

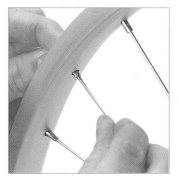  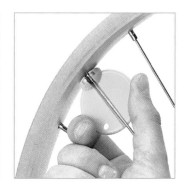

3 Remove the rim tape and pull out the rest of the old spoke. Unscrew the nipple on the new spoke and bend it slightly so that you can thread the end into the spoke hole. Check that the spoke head is still seated correctly.

4 Do the nipple up finger tight and check that the new spoke is following exactly the same route as the old ones. If the rim has angled seats, make sure you tighten the nipple right down into the base of the insert.

5 Twang the spokes with your fingers to get an idea of how tight they are. Then progressively tighten the new spoke until it's under the same tension as the rest. File off the end of the spoke if necessary and true up the wheel.

Chapter 8

BARS & SADDLES

When on a bike, most of your weight is taken by your hands and seat. Your feet take very little. For maximum comfort, tailor your handlebars and saddle so that the weight falls equally on them both.

Components and care

In the drive to save weight, lots of new materials and ways of joining them together are being used in bike manufacture. But as these bikes get older, problems may emerge.

Rust and corrosion on iron and steel are easy to spot. But it seldom becomes a problem on bikes because steel frames and components have plenty of strength in reserve. It's possible to imagine a frame becoming fatally weakened by rust, but it seldom if ever happens in practice.

Aluminum alloy also corrodes, but it's hard to spot because the white flecks of oxide blend in with the silver color of the metal. In normal conditions, corrosion stops at the surface of the metal. But handlebar stems and seat posts are a very tight fit in the frame and so the aluminum and steel come into close contact. If water gets into this area, it forms an electrical connection between the two different metals, and corrosion can then go very fast.

You can combat this effect by using anti-seize wherever different metals come into contact. But despite this, you should check highly stressed alloy components like seat posts and stems. If you find serious pitting in the surface of the aluminum, consider replacing the component, because alloy bike parts don't have the reserve strength of steel.

Welded components can also fail, particularly stems where a lot of stress is concentrated on small areas of weld. If it's been overheated, the metal surrounding the weld can crack. And if impurities have got in, pin holes will form in the weld itself. Throw away any component showing these problems.

1 Welded stems have become popular in the last few years. As they get older, there is a possibility that problems may emerge. Check the weld bead and the surrounding metal for pin holes and cracks.

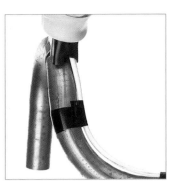

2 Handlebars are made from very thin gauge tubing. If the brake lever band starts to cut into the metal, cracks may fan out from that point. Check whenever you remove the handlebar tape, just in case.

3 Handlebars can also crack if the metal has been fatigued by too many heavy landings. It's most likely to happen to ultra-light components, and the most likely spot is where the handlebar bulges.

VARIATIONS
Tailoring your riding position can go way beyond adjusting your saddle and handlebar height. Reach can be adjusted by installing a stem with a shorter or longer extension as well as by altering the position of the saddle. You can also install handlebars of a different width. With drop handlebars, the shape and drop can also be varied to suit the rider.

4 Three problems are likely to affect the seat post. First is crumbly white corrosion. Second is the saddle clamp cutting into the seat post. Third is overtightening of the seat bolt clamp. Replace if you find any of these problems.

5 Stems and seat posts are both marked with a line to show the maximum amount that is allowed to stick out of the frame. If there is no line, assume that at least one third of the length should always be left in the frame.

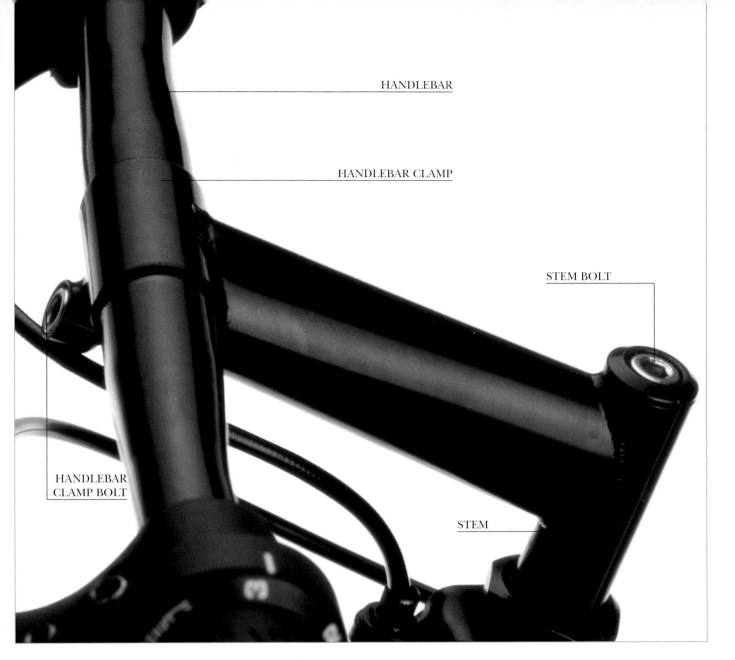

HANDLEBAR

HANDLEBAR CLAMP

STEM BOLT

HANDLEBAR
CLAMP BOLT

STEM

6 Aheadset and Tioga stems can be identified by their painted trade-marks. The stem is part of the headset and cannot be adjusted in the normal way. See Chapter 9 for details of this system found on many mountain bikes.

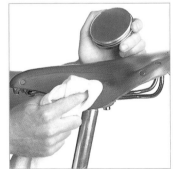

7 Solid leather saddles must be allowed to dry out naturally, whenever they get wet. If the rain soaks right into the saddle, apply a dressing to feed the leather and build up water resistance. Tighten the nose bolt if the leather sags.

WHEN YOU NEED TO DO THIS JOB
◆ As part of a major overhaul.
◆ If you spot any crumbly white corrosion, particularly around the top of the headset.
◆ When you're doing an overhaul on a newly acquired secondhand bike, particularly if it's long in the tooth.

TIME
◆ 5 minutes to check everything except the handlebars as they're usually covered with tape.

DIFFICULTY
◆ It's quite easy to spot any cracks or corrosion and you shouldn't underestimate the chances of a component failing after a number of years.

NO SPECIAL TOOLS NEEDED

Handlebars and stems

Although they come in many shapes and sizes, nearly all handlebars and stems go together and fit on a bike in the same way.

Whether on expensive racers or on budget utilities, handlebars fit into a clamp at the front of the stem while the stem itself is held into the frame with a binder bolt. Apart, that is, from recent mountain bikes with the Aheadset/Tioga system. Yet even with this, the way the handlebars are attached to the stem remains unchanged although the stem installation and adjustment are quite different. Check the section covering this point in Chapter 10.

The binder bolt works in two ways. Sometimes it screws into a cone which is drawn up inside the stem, causing it to expand and lock in position inside the frame. The more common type screws into a wedge which also locks the stem into place.

You will only occasionally want to put on new handlebars or a new stem. But you can alter the angle of the handlebars just by loosening the clamp bolt, making the change and then tightening it up again. The height of the handlebars is altered by undoing the binder bolt, dislodging the wedge with a hammer, raising or lowering the handlebars and tightening the bolt up again. If the handlebars won't move after you've dislodged the wedge, hold the front wheel between your knees and twist them from side to side as you lift them. You can only alter the reach by installing a different stem.

The curves on drop handlebars are often very tight and make it difficult to slide them in and out of the handlebar clamp. It's sometimes possible to open up the handlebar clamp by reversing the clamp bolt, but, more commonly, you have to drive a cold chisel or heavy screwdriver into the gap. Be careful as there is a chance of the clamp cracking.

If you're riding with flat handlebars and they're too wide, you can narrow them down with a hacksaw or, better, a plumber's pipe cutter, obtainable from your local hardware shop.

Removing stem and handlebars

1 Undo the binder bolt at the top of the stem five or six turns. On some there is a standard bolt head, but most recent stems have an Allen key fitting. The bolt head may be hidden by a rubber plug which you have to pry out for access.

2 You still won't be able to move the stem, because the wedge stays in place after the bolt is loosened. You have to dislodge it with a sharp blow from a hammer and it should move. If it doesn't, protect the bolt head with a piece of wood before you hit it again.

Adjusting and changing handlebars

1 To change the handlebars, start off by removing the brake levers, gear levers, light brackets and so on. But if you're just altering the angle of the bars or taking them off temporarily along with the stem, don't bother.

2 Now undo the handlebar clamp bolt. You only need to loosen it a few turns to adjust the position of the bars, but remove the bolt completely if you are separating bars from stem. In a few cases, the clamp has two smaller bolts.

THEY DON'T ALWAYS MIX AND MATCH
In a perfect world, every make of handlebar would fit every make of stem. Unfortunately, although handlebars are identical in principle, different makers work to different sizes. So you may have to use a lot of force to open up the handlebar clamp or accept heavy scratching when separating them.

3 You will find the stem is still a tight fit in the frame, so grip the front wheel between your legs and wrench the handlebars from side to side at the same time as you pull them upwards. When replacing, coat the lower part of the stem and the wedge with anti-seize.

4 On some stems, the top is closed off with a large rubber plug, but, when you pull it out, you should be able to see the Allen head a little way below. (Don't confuse this type of stem with the Aheadset type. On these you will see a small Allen bolt on top of the stem.)

5 The Allen head is buried so deep in this type of stem that you will only be able to reach it with the long end of an Allen key. Slip a narrow piece of tubing over the short end of the Allen key so that you will have enough leverage to undo the binder bolt.

WHEN YOU NEED TO DO THIS JOB
◆ After putting on a new saddle or changing its position.
◆ If you are not comfortable.

TIME
◆ 30 minutes to install new handlebars.
◆ 5 minutes to reposition stem or handlebars.

DIFFICUTY 🔧🔧🔧🔧
◆ It can be quite difficult to remove the handlebars without scratching.

3 You can now try to work the handlebars out of the clamp. Be careful as there is sometimes a separate metal sleeve around the handlebars, inside the clamp. Don't hurry as it's only too easy to scratch the bars badly.

4 If it's impossible to pull the handlebars out of the stem, try replacing the clamp bolt the opposite way with a coin in the slot. As you tighten the bolt, it will open up the clamp, but it only works when the bolt hole is threaded.

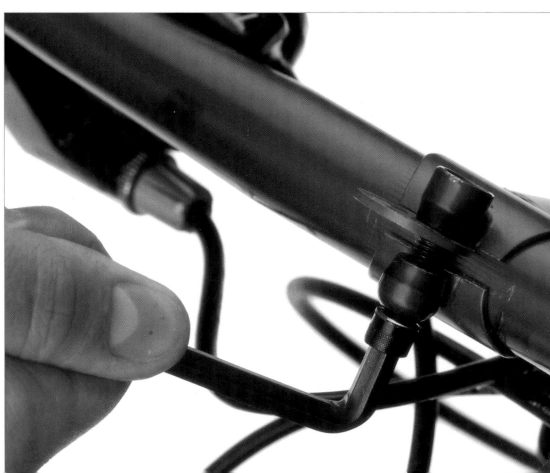

Grips and tape

Nothing ages a bike more than a battered set of handgrips or torn and dirty handlebar tape. Luckily, replacements cost very little.

Nearly all new mountain bikes are sold with flat handlebars, and, to make sure they fit everybody, they're quite wide. This is OK on short journeys, but it forces most riders to use a spread-arm riding position that can be tiring. If you're installing new grips, this is a good moment to consider whether you'd be more comfortable with narrower handlebars or with bar ends that give you a completely different hand position.

The cheapest way to get narrower handlebars is simply to cut a few inches off the ends. But before you do this, check that it will leave enough room for the brake levers and shifters. One way to cut a few inches off is to saw through the handlebars with a hacksaw and then clean up the ends with a file. But you'll get a better job if you use a plumber's pipe cutter. This has a hardened disc and you just wind it around the bar until it cuts right through.

There are many different types and styles of bar end but the less expensive styles made of aluminum suit most riders. When you're fitting them to alloy handlebars, don't overtighten the clamp bolt or the aluminum tube may collapse under the pressure.

You don't have to use rubber grips on a mountain bike. You can instead use handlebar tape, as used on nearly all road bikes. This is available in various materials and lots of different colors and patterns. The most popular handlebar tape is slightly padded plastic, but you can get cork, which gives a cool sweat-free grip, and cloth. Cloth ages fast, but it always feels good. When you reach the brake levers with the tape, use its natural stretch to mold the tape neatly around the clip and the hood.

Top-quality racing bike handlebars have a groove for the brake cables. Use a few short lengths of tape to fix the brake cable in the groove before you apply the main covering.

WHEN YOU NEED TO DO THIS JOB
◆ Grips and tape are old and worn.
◆ Handlebars feel too wide.
◆ You want to add bar ends to give a more comfortable ride.

TIME
◆ 15 minutes to install new grips.
◆ 20 minutes to cut down handlebars with pipe cutter and move brake levers – 5 minutes more with hacksaw.
◆ 15 minutes to remove old handlebar tape and install new.

DIFFICULTY
◆ Pretty easy, even if you have to reduce handlebar width.

SPECIAL TOOLS
◆ Plumber's pipe cutter.

Adding bar ends

1 If you intend keeping the same handgrips, lightly tap the end of the rubber grip with a hammer or mallet. The hammer head should be larger in diameter than the handgrip.

2 As you tap the bar end, the handlebar will cut through the rubber of the handgrip. Once it's been cut through in a couple of places, finish the job off neatly with a utility knife.

Taping drop handlebars

1 Pull out the handlebar end plugs first. Some have a central screw which must be loosened first to ease off the pressure, but most just pull out or pry out with a screwdriver.

2 Undo all the old tape, cutting it with a utility knife if necessary. Then roll back the rubber brake hood and use a short length of tape to cover the edge of the lever.

New grips for flat bars

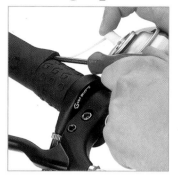

1 If the old grips are finished, just cut them off. If you want to reuse them, open up the grip with a screwdriver, fire some spray lube into the gap and pull them off.

2 You will probably have to twist and pull the grips at the same time to drag them off. Underneath, the bar will be covered in slime, so wipe it clean with a cloth.

3 Remove the old bar ends and spray the grip part of the handlebars with ordinary hairspray. Now slide the new grip on immediately, before the hairspray dries.

4 If you've no hairspray, use aerosol paint. When necessary, use the palm of your hand to push the grip along the handlebar but move fast or it will stick in the wrong place.

3 With the end of the grip out of the way, you should be able to twist and push the handgrip down the handlebar, giving a short length of bare metal to mount the bar end to.

4 The bar end should now fit, but it may be necessary to remove the bolt and open the mounting hole up with a screwdriver. Then tighten the bolt, but not too hard.

3 Start installing the tape close to the center of the handlebars, overlapping it carefully and stretching it around the brake levers. When you get to the end, tuck it in neatly.

4 Add new bar end plugs as a final touch. Sometimes they go in easily but you may have to use the palm of your hand to screw them round and round until they fit flush.

Saddles with saddle clamp

Although they are simple in principle, saddle clamps are very difficult to put back on to a saddle once you've taken them off.

There is normally no need to separate saddle clamp from saddle. But if you've had to do so for some reason, re-assemble all the parts in the correct order on the through bolt. Then hold everything in place by tightening both nuts an equal amount to ensure that the through bolt stays centered in the clip. Finger tighten the nuts only.

Make sure the saddle rail retainers face outwards and slip them on to the saddle rails from the rear. If necessary, loosen the nuts a little so that you can turn the outer washers until they also fit on the saddle rails. Retighten the nuts as soon as possible afterwards.

With the clamp fitted to the saddle fairly loosely, you can now fit the clamp on to the slimmer section of the seat post. The clamp will slide backwards and forwards on the rails to help you get a comfortable position, and you can also change the angle of the saddle. This is best done by loosening both nuts a little at a time until they're loose enough to allow the ridges on the serrated saddle clamp and saddle rail retainers to jump over each other and then retightening the nuts as soon as soon as you've completed the adjustment.

Don't mount the circular part of the saddle clamp right at the base of the seat post as it could eventually saw right through, causing the saddle to drop off!

You will find more information on seat posts on pages 138 and 139.

SADDLE

SADDLE RAILS

SEAT POST

SADDLE CLAMP

SEAT POST BINDER BOLT

Final saddle adjustment

1 It's very important to get the angle of the saddle right, otherwise most of your weight will rest on the most sensitive part of your anatomy. You first undo the nut on one side of the saddle clamp.

2 Don't undo the nuts too much or it will be impossible to make fine adjustments to the saddle angle. To tilt the nose downwards, lean on the front of the saddle and lift the back with your hand.

3 To tilt the saddle nose upwards, lift on the front and lean down on the back. But remember, the saddle should always be either horizontal or slightly nose up, never nose down.

4 A saddle clamp also allows adjustment backwards and forwards. Loosen the nut slightly on one side and thump the back of the saddle with the heel of your hand to move it forwards and vice versa.

5 When you think you've got the adjustment right, tighten the nut up very hard and test ride. If the adjustment is badly out, you will soon feel it, but only a long ride will reveal the full picture.

WHEN YOU NEED TO DO THIS JOB
◆ Fitting a saddle to a standard seat post, usually on an older type of bike.
◆ Swapping a saddle from a new bike to an old one.
◆ Adjusting the riding position.

TIME
◆ Fitting a saddle clamp could take 5 minutes or drive you mad and take 15 minutes.
◆ Adjusting saddle height is easy, unless the seat post is stuck in the frame.

DIFFICULTY 🔧🔧🔧🔧
◆ It's one of those jobs where you feel you need three hands – one to hold the clamp, one to hold the saddle and the other to use the wrench. But if you can't move the saddle up or down, try spray lube. You may find it easier if you assemble the clamp away from the saddle and fit it back on all in one piece. If that doesn't work, see a bike mechanic.

NO SPECIAL TOOLS NEEDED

Raising and removing saddle

SEAT POST HEIGHT
Most seat posts are marked with a line showing the minimum length which should be inside the frame at any time. To put it another way, you should never see the line on the seat post when the bike is in use. As a rule of thumb, you should keep one third of the length inside the frame.

1 Saddle height is adjusted by undoing the seat post binder bolt until it is fairly loose. If the seat post is a tight fit in the frame, it won't move easily. You have to turn it from side to side to get it to move.

2 Turn the saddle two or three inches each way and lean on it to adjust downwards. And to raise the saddle, move it from side to side and lift at the same time. Tighten binder bolt hard when it's right.

3 Whenever you take out the seat post, wipe it with a cloth and check inside the frame tube for corrosion. When you're replacing the seat post, coat lightly with anti-seize to ensure that it doesn't rust.

137

Saddles with micro-adjuster

Seat posts with a built-in clamp are neat and light, but some have more fore-and-aft adjustment than others.

Nearly all mountain bikes and most recent racing bikes have a seat post with a built-in saddle clamp. Most have a good range of adjustment, but it varies between different types and you may have to install another make to get a perfect riding position.

There are many variations on the basic design and some of them are not strictly micro-adjusting. Others have a two-bolt design which necessitates loosening one bolt and tightening the other to adjust the saddle angle. This is an even better arrangement than the standard design.

Seat posts have two important dimensions – diameter and length. Diameter is the more critical because there are at least four standard sizes and really no way of telling which one is correct, apart from measuring the old one. If you try to fit the wrong seat post, it will either seize in place and possibly destroy the frame, or it will be loose and the saddle will collapse under you some day. If in doubt about the correct size, it's not good enough to measure the old seat post yourself with a ruler. Take it instead to a bike shop and make sure they measure it with either callipers or a micrometer.

Road bikes have a standard seat post length of 180 mm. Mountain bikes generally use longer seat posts – up to 300 mm in length to compensate for the smaller frame sizes.

SADDLE

SADDLE RAILS

CRADLE

SEAT POST

CLAMP BOLT

SEAT POST QUICK RELEASE CLAMP

eat post

CREAKING NOISES

It's quite common for a saddle to make creaking noises, most often when you're climbing a hill or sprinting. If this annoys you, try a light coat of anti-seize on the clamp bolt plus the cradle and clamp. Don't be tempted to overtighten the clamp bolt as it might snap.

WHEN YOU NEED TO DO THIS JOB

◆ When installing a new saddle or seat post.
◆ To adjust your riding position.

TIME

◆ 10 minutes to mount a new saddle or seat post.
◆ 2 minutes to make a change to the saddle position.

DIFFICULTY

◆ You should find this very much easier than working on a saddle with its own clamp, whether you're installing a new seat post or adjusting the position of the saddle.

NO SPECIAL TOOLS NEEDED

1 On the standard design single bolt seat post, the saddle clamp is held in place by a bolt through the cradle. In the type shown, the cradle is part of the seat post, but it's usually separate. Always use anti-seize on the clamp bolt.

2 When you want to remove the saddle, just undo the clamp bolt until the saddle clamp is very loose. The clamp bolt is usually made of soft aluminum, sometimes even titanium, so make sure you use a tightly fitting Allen key.

3 If you turn the saddle clamp around, you can now lift the saddle out of the cradle. When replacing the saddle, you'll probably have to fiddle with the saddle clamp for a bit to get it correctly positioned on both saddle rails.

4 It's very easy to adjust the saddle fore and aft. Just loosen the clamp bolt a little and tap it backwards or forwards with the heel of your hand. There is a wide range of adjustment, so don't forget the basic advice on riding position.

5 Angle adjustment is more difficult. First, loosen off the clamp bolt a little more and then tilt the whole thing – saddle, cradle and clamp – up or down. Try holding the clamp with your fingers to retain the basic position.

6 When you're satisfied with the new saddle position, check that it's properly aligned with the top tube of the frame. Loosen the seat post clamp and correct if necessary. Finally, test ride to make sure you're comfortable.

SEAT POST QUICK RELEASE

Lots of mountain bikes have a seat post quick release instead of a bolt. It's similar to the quick release on a hub, so, when you tighten the lever, it should require a definite effort to lock it. If it doesn't, tighten the nut on the opposite side from the lever. Once you get used to whipping the seat post in and out, you will find it's a useful security device. It also makes it easier to load your bike in a car.

CHAPTER 9

FRAME & FORKS

Whether they're intended for crossing ploughed fields or climbing
Alpine passes, nearly all bikes have a diamond frame made up of two
linked triangles plus the forks. The sizes of the tubes and the angles
between them may vary but they're all sisters under the skin.

Frame materials and design

Fully assembled bikes are such good value that it's not worth buying a separate frame and fitting the components yourself, unless you're going for a top-of-the-range machine.

Top-of-the-range frames are built from exotic materials like carbon fiber and titanium or, increasingly, from aluminum. But when you're working within a budget, steel remains the best all round choice for a frame material and that applies to mountain bikes, utilities and road bikes.

The best-known maker of bike tubing is Reynolds which gives its tube sets numbers. The range starts with the budget 501 tube set and goes up to the top quality 853, although the well known 531 remains the least expensive high-quality tubing on the market.

Columbus, the big Italian tube supplier, mostly uses names for its tube sets. Gara is fairly inexpensive, Aelle is mid-range while SL and SLX are high quality.

The Japanese firm Tange supplies tubing to many American and Taiwanese bike builders but doesn't have a clear range structure like Reynolds and Columbus. These makers also use True Temper tube sets made in America. On the whole, you get what you pay for from the big mountain bike manufacturers and frame quality nearly always goes hand in hand with the quality of the components.

Bike frames are all based on triangles and this concentrates the stresses where one tube is joined to the next. So good-quality frame tubing is drawn thicker at the ends where the stresses build up and thinner in the middle, to save weight. The thick ends are called butts and the tubes are spoken of as single butted if only one end is thicker and double butted if both ends are manufactured like this. Nearly all good-quality tube sets are double butted.

Apart from the tubing, the other factors in frame quality are the method used to join the tubes together and workmanship.

Lugs are the traditional way of joining tubes. They're metal sleeves slightly larger in diameter than the tubes. The gap between tube and lug is filled with molten brass to hold everything in place. The only thing that can go wrong is that if the tubing is overheated while it's being brazed, it can become weak or brittle. On the whole, the lugs should get thinner as the tube quality goes up. Don't buy a frame with quality tubing and clumsy-looking lugs.

Welded frames are usually built using the TIG method. This process is automated and enables the big bike makers to produce lightweight frames of consistently high quality, in very large numbers. In TIG and similar processes, the welding head is surrounded with inert gas to cool the weld and prevent the molten metal from being attacked by oxygen from the atmosphere. The welding machine should produce an even-looking bead of weld with a regular pattern of overlapping ridges. Don't buy a frame if the bead looks clumsy or has pinholes in it.

Utility Bikes

Utility bikes are built from heavy carbon steel tubing and the whole frame leans backwards to give a relaxed, upright riding position. The forks are very long to give a comfortable ride and stable though slow steering.

Mountain or 'Hybrid' Bikes

Any reasonable quality hybrid, as shown here, or mountain bike is built with chrome molybdenum lightweight tubing. The top tube slopes – if not from aluminum – to make it easier for the rider to get his or her feet down.

1 On welded frames, you can usually spot the tell-tale rough line of welding in the angle between each tube. But the best frame builders finish their work so carefully that one tube appears to blend seamlessly into the next.

2 Composite – usually carbon fiber – frames have this same seamless quality. You can tell they aren't metal because the tubes don't ring when you flick them with your finger and the joints are often reinforced with webs or gussets.

3 Suspension forks are now almost standard on MTBs used for serious off-road work. If you're buying new and want to upgrade to suspension forks later, check that the frame geometry will let you to do this without upsetting the handling.

4 Built-in gear hangers indicate that you're looking at a reasonable-quality frame, on a road bike or an MTB. If two sets of bottle mounts and well-thought-out cable guides are fitted, it confirms you're looking at a reasonable product.

5 Traditional frames built with tubes from Reynolds or Columbus are still hard to beat for road use. Check that the lugs which hold the frame together blend into the tubes and that there are plenty of brazed-on fittings.

6 If a frame builder manages to arrange the seat stays, two main tubes and the seat post clamp in a neat but strong looking cluster, the chances are that they know their business.

Road Bikes

Quality road racing bikes are often built of light manganese steel tubing. Upright frame angles position the rider over the crankset for pedalling efficiency and the forks are fairly short for quick steering.

Frame inspection and crash repair

Bike frames are strong but a serious crash can kink the tubes or put the whole thing out of kilter. You won't always be able to spot the damage but it's worth a try.

Luckily, most bike frames have plenty of reserve strength, but it's not unknown for them to go out of alignment. When this happens, the wheels will lie at different angles to each other and the bike won't steer straight. Sometimes you'll be able to spot this by eye, especially if you check the frame from different directions and compare the appearance from the front and the back. If you begin to suspect that the alignment is out, have the frame checked professionally.

Watch out also for damage to the seat stays that run between the back wheel and the saddle. On any frame they're the narrowest tubes of all and so the most likely to be bent.

Most frames have several brazed-on fittings. If you find any difficulty getting the rear derailleur mounting bolt or the gear lever tensioning bolt into the thread, have them cleaned out with a tap by a professional bike mechanic. This is most likely to happen to the rear derailleur hanger as it has a very coarse thread.

WHEN YOU NEED TO DO THIS JOB
◆ When buying second-hand.
◆ After a crash.
◆ If you feel the bike isn't running straight.

TIME
◆ 10 minutes is enough for a thorough inspection from several different angles. Always try to look along the frame against the light.

DIFFICULTY 𝄖𝄖𝄖
◆ When you first start, you will think you're going cross-eyed, but you will soon get the hang of it.

NO SPECIAL TOOLS

Checking for

1 Position yourself at the front of the bike and look along the frame. You should be able to see if the short head tube and the seat tube that carries the saddle line up.

3 Now look along the frame from the back. The rear derailleur should hang down straight and the seat tube align with the head tube. Make sure also that the seat stays are straight and undamaged.

5 Finally, run your fingers along the underside of all the tubes because when looking from the top or side, you can easily miss serious damage. The top and down tubes nearly always go in a bad smash.

Straightening a gear hanger

The first thing to hit the ground in a crash is often the rear derailleur and sometimes the gear hanger gets bent as well. If the damage is severe, it's possible to have a complete new dropout fitted by a professional frame repairer. But it isn't cheap and you may be able to fix things yourself. First, check that the bottom half of the dropout is correctly aligned with the top. Then fit an adjustable wrench over the dropout so that it bridges the two halves and bend the hanger straight. When you bend the metal, do it in one slow continuous movement using steady pressure.

144

crash damage

2 Stand over the bike looking down. You'll be able to see if the horizontal top tube lines up with the diagonal down tube. Check also that the forks splay out an equal amount.

4 Run your fingers down the back and front of the forks, checking for ripples in the tubing. Check also that the fork curves look smooth and drop the front wheel out, so you can see if it fits back in easily.

6 You might easily miss crash damage to the forks or tubes when making a purely visual inspection – for example the tiny ripples in the tubes shown right. Your sense of touch will often pick up this sort of damage better than your eyes, so take care to run your fingertips along the underside of all the tubes. Neither tubes nor welds have cracked here, showing the amazing strength of a really well-built frame.

Standard headset

Stripping and greasing a headset is easy, but leave installing a new one to a professional mechanic.

When a bike is past its first youth, you may find that the steering is no longer as free as it should be. This might be because the headset needs an overhaul. But when you go over a bump, the bearing race on top of the forks lifts and smashes the ball bearings into the bottom ball race. At the same time, the top bearing race is lifted away from the bearings, so they don't get battered as badly. After this has happened a few thousand times, depressions are formed in the bottom races which the ball bearings have to climb in and out of when you turn the handlebars. This makes the steering feel stiff and as if there are notches that hold the steering column at different points on its rotation. This can only be put right by installing a new headset.

If you ride a bike with the headset loose, it increases the force with which the ball bearings smash into the races and speeds up wear. So when the front brakes start chattering, check for play in the headset and adjust immediately.

WHEN YOU NEED TO DO THIS JOB
◆ The bike is in for a general overhaul.
◆ There is a chattering when you turn a sharp corner or apply the brakes hard.
◆ Turning the handlebars requires effort.

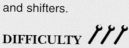

TIME
◆ 30 minutes if you just lift the handlebars.
◆ 40 minutes if you decide to remove the brake levers and shifters.

DIFFICULTY

◆ It's not too difficult to strip down, grease and adjust a headset, especially if you've got suitable spanners. Don't try installing a complete new headset because it requires special tools.

SPECIAL TOOLS
◆ Headset spanners.

1 If you're stripping and greasing a headset, you may be able to get away with lifting the handlebars out of the frame and letting them hang there. But it can be easier to remove the forks if you remove the brake levers and shifters.

2 Your first move is to undo the locknut. A tight-fitting spanner is best but an adjustable wrench will do. Most quality bikes have a soft alloy headset which you'll probably damage if you don't use a headset spanner.

3 Below the locknut is the spacer washer. In some cases, the steerer tube has a flat on one side and there is a matching flat on the spacer. If the bike is fitted with center-pull brakes, the brake cable hanger also fits in here.

5 Gather up the ball bearings. Some will probably be stuck in the top cup, others on top of the forks. Clean everything up with solvent and inspect all four bearing races for signs of wear, particularly the bottom bearing cup and fork race.

6 Stick new ball bearings in the top and bottom cups with waterproof grease. Don't use caged bearings. Fit the fork back in the frame and screw down the top race to hold it there. Then adjust the top race to eliminate any play.

7 Fit the lockwasher and screw the locknut down on it. Now apply the front brake and see if you can feel any movement. If you can't detect it this way, try wedging your finger between bottom race and fork crown.

LOCKNUT

LOCK WASHER

TOP BEARING RACE

HEAD TUBE

BOTTOM
BEARING CUP

FORK RACE

FORK

4 Unscrew the top race next.
If the bike is standing on
the floor, the steerer tube
won't move. But if you have a
workstand, the forks will drop
out as you undo the top race.
Take care the ball bearings
don't drop all over the floor.

8 Check that there is minimum friction at the handlebars but no movement in the
bearing. When it's right, hold
the top race with one spanner
and tighten the locknut against
it with the other. Test ride and
readjust if necessary.

Aheadset and Tioga headsets

Many recent mountain bikes have a stem, headset and forks designed as a single set of components, saving quite a bit of weight.

All the parts in this type of headset are held together by the stem. This in turn is clamped to the steerer tube on the forks. You adjust the free play in the steering by increasing or decreasing the pressure of the stem on the top bearing race. If the stem doesn't move freely up and down the steerer tube, you won't be able to set up the headset bearings correctly.

To adjust the bearings, undo the pinch bolt and tighten or loosen the Allen screw until there is no play in the steering but it turns with a minimum amount of effort. Re-tighten the pinch bolt and check adjustment by applying the front brake and seeing if there is any movement detectable at the handlebars. Readjust the Allen bolt if necessary.

1 The top cap of the headset is held in place with an Allen bolt which also screws into a special nut inside the steerer tube. Standard caps are designed to break if you over-tighten the Allen bolt, so don't install non-standard ones.

2 Lift the cap off the stem next. Check that it's marked with the same brand name as the stem, not the name of a bike accessory maker. If you look down inside the stem, you'll see the special nut inside the steerer tube.

3 Now undo the pinch bolt holding the stem to the steerer tube. Sometimes there is just one pinch bolt, sometimes a pair at the back of the stem. But the latest design has a single pinch bolt buried in the front of the stem.

4 Once you've removed the pinch bolt, you can lift the stem off the steerer tube. But when you've done that, there is nothing holding the fork into the frame and it could fall out if you don't hold it in place with your hand.

6 The top bearing race is now free, so lift it off and put it to one side. Then raise the front of the bike, allowing the fork to drop out. Ask a helper to hold the fork while you check the bottom bearing cup and fork race for wear and pitting.

7 Clean up all components, put new ball bearings in the cups and reassemble by reversing the previous steps. Coat all surfaces with anti-seize as you do so and check that the stem moves up and down freely. Then adjust the free play.

WHEN YOU NEED TO DO THIS JOB
◆ During a major overhaul.
◆ If the steering is stiff or notchy.
◆ When the forks seem to chatter in the frame.

TIME
◆ 30 minutes. As this type of headset is simpler to work on, you probably don't need to take the brake levers and shifters off.

DIFFICULTY 🔧🔧🔧
◆ The hardest thing about this job is understanding how it all goes together. But make sure that you clean everything carefully as the stem must slide up and down freely.

NO SPECIAL TOOLS NEEDED

PINCH BOLT

HANDLEBAR SPACER

TOP BEARING RACE

CABLE HANGER

HEAD TUBE

5 There may be spacer washers and a brake cable hanger under the stem. Lift them off and locate the conical washer that locks the top bearing race to the steerer tube. Pry it out and lift it off.

BOTTOM BEARING CUP

TIOGA HEADSETS

Tioga headsets are very similar in principle to the headsets shown here. However, they usually have a circlip, which is a circular spring device that fits in a groove, to hold the forks in the frame. Before you can remove the top bearing race, you will find that it is necessary to remove the circlip by prying it off with a screwdriver or by opening it up with circlip pliers.

BIKE EXTRAS

Bikes do a hundred different jobs but they will do most of them better with some carefully chosen additions. Just be careful you don't turn your lightweight into a heavyweight.

Lighting

The majority of bikes don't have any provision for lights, and riders try to get home before dark. But a certain amount of preparation will turn a bike into a perfectly safe 24-hour machine.

Legally, your bike must be equipped with a white front light and a red rear one when you ride after dark. In addition, reflectors are a good idea. An even better attention-getter is a flashing light, available with a choice of red or white lenses. The light is generated electronically with a diode, which is vastly more efficient than a filament bulb. So although tiny, the batteries have a long life.

Battery-powered lights are the cheapest way of complying with the law, and, in conjunction with high-power halogen bulbs, they're quite bright until the batteries start to fade. Unfortunately, they fade fast. Regular night riders often use rechargeable batteries to get around this problem. Batteries last longer with standard tungsten bulbs.

Various generator lights use the rider's own energy to produce electricity to power the lighting. The commonest variety runs off the side of the tire but there is an argument that the roller tends to slip. To prevent this, some generators are mounted under the bottom bracket. In this position it's possible to use a much larger, slip-resistant roller. However, all generator lights suffer from the major shortcoming that the light stops when the bike stops, unless you go to the additional complication and expense of installing back-up batteries.

Maybe the best solution for regular winter bike riders is the rechargeable battery which fits in a bottle cage. The lights are connected to this battery with electrical wire. When the lights dim or as part of a weekly routine, you recharge the battery as you would a car battery.

Better battery lighting

1 Battery powered lights are susceptible to the bike environment. Water can get inside and cause the batteries to corrode. As a result they need regular care. The first step is to unscrew the case to gain access to the battery and bulb.

2 Remove the batteries and inspect the contacts. Check for dampness, green corrosion and red rust. Clean and remove any deposits with emery paper. Remove the batteries completely if the lights are not to be used for a long period of time.

WHEN YOU NEED TO DO THIS JOB
◆ Your battery lights flicker or have stopped.

TIME
◆ 15 minutes to strip and clean a battery lamp.

DIFFICULTY ✹✹✹
◆ Sometimes it's difficult to get at all the bare copper connections inside the lamp and clean them up.

NO SPECIAL TOOLS NEEDED

Mounting a generator

1 Fit the generator mounting around the fork blade so the roller lines up with the file pattern on the tire wall. Then loosen the angle bolt and adjust the position of the generator until the roller forms a right angle with the spokes.

2 Remove the paint on the frame under the grounding screw on the mounting clip, coat with petroleum jelly and refit. Ground the lights in the same way. Then run the wires to the front and rear lights, keeping them as short as possible.

3 Most modern battery lights are fitted with halogen bulbs which provide a very strong beam. To replace the bulb, remove the lens case taking note of how it came off as some only fit on one way.

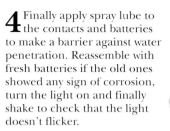

4 Finally apply spray lube to the contacts and batteries to make a barrier against water penetration. Reassemble with fresh batteries if the old ones showed any sign of corrosion, turn the light on and finally shake to check that the light doesn't flicker.

3 To prevent wiring problems, attach all wires neatly to the frame with zip ties. Apply spray lube to the connections and tighten lightly with a wrench if necessary. Road test downhill to check the rear bulb doesn't burn out.

4 All bikes are safer with a flashing diode rear light. But they're particularly good with a generator as the normal rear light won't work when you're standing still. Flashing lights can be attached to your clothing or bike.

A FEW REFLECTIONS
Bike lights are tiny and weak in comparison with all the other sources of light on the road, so they get swallowed up by car headlights and so on. Luckily, reflective materials are highly effective and throw a large patch of brightly colored light back at drivers. Best of all are the reflective arm and leg bands which are always moving, alerting the doziest driver to the fact that you are on the road and need room to maneuver in.

Mudguards and carriers

There is only one thing worse than a bike with mudguards on a sunny day and that's a bike without mudguards on a wet one.

Bikes lend themselves to many things, but somehow the basic design, with large wheels stuck out at each end, makes it very difficult to mount satisfactory mudguards. They frequently need fiddling with to keep them rattle-free and prevent them from rubbing on the tires.

It's particularly difficult to put mudguards on a mountain bike, especially if you're going to use it in muddy conditions. There are lots of different designs, but they're nearly all snap-on plastic devices that only divert the worst of the spray.

On most road bikes, the problem is that the mudguard bridge is only made of soft alloy so that you can easily fold it around the mudguard with your thumbs. It's then bolted to the brake bridge that fits between the seat stays, sharing it with the back brake. If this is a sidepull, you have to somehow center the brake and the mudguard, hold them both in the correct place and do up the bolt.

Cantilever brakes, as in the steps shown here, are not bolted to the brake bridge, so it's easier to install a mudguard in this case. Failing that, consider putting on dual pivot brakes as they're easier to center.

There is a bit of an art in adjusting mudguards but the main thing to grasp is that it's usually best to adjust the side that's too far from the tire. If it's a long way out, loosen the mudguard eye and slide the mudguard up or down as necessary. But if it's just a minor problem, try putting a slight bend in the mudguard stay. It won't be noticed and it's easy to straighten out again if necessary.

For neatness and strength, use Allen screws to attach the mudguard stays and the carrier to the frame, bearing in mind that the carrier may take quite a load. Use self-locking nuts to stop them from working loose again. And if you are buying a bike and expect to install a carrier and a mudguard, look for a frame with separate mudguard and carrier mountings at the back. Mudguards can be fitted to road frames without mudguard eyelets, using special fittings.

1 Unhook the back brake, hold the mudguard up to the back wheel and mark the position of the brake bridge. Fit the mudguard bridge so that the mounting loop aligns with the brake bridge.

2 Push the mudguard under the seat stay bridge and adjust the position of the mudguard bridge so it touches the front. Fit the wire stays into the mudguard eyelets and attach to the frame with screws.

4 Reconnect the brake and bolt the mudguard bridge to the seat stay bridge. Use a self-locking nut to prevent the bolt from coming loose. Tighten up the tabs on the mudguard bridge with pliers.

5 Adjust the stays so that the mudguards are evenly spaced around the tire. You can do this either by bending the stays to correct small problems or by adjusting the mudguard fittings if it's miles out.

WHEN YOU NEED TO DO THIS JOB

◆ You want to ride, rain or shine.
◆ You're going touring and need mudguards in case of rain plus a carrier for your luggage.

TIME

◆ At least an hour to install mudguards really carefully. It's best to take your time with this job.

DIFFICULTY

◆ It can be frustrating, trying to get everything right.

NO SPECIAL TOOLS NEEDED

3 Adjust the position of the mudguard so that it's evenly spaced around the wheel. You may find it easier to do this if you tighten one or two of the eye bolts temporarily while you get the others right.

6 Bolt the bottom carrier mountings to the frame via the mudguard eyelets or the carrier mountings, if there are separate ones. Then fix to the top mountings, if any, or to the seat stays.

7 Once you've added a carrier, you can carry some things using an elastic luggage strap, but pannier bags allow you to carry much more. Ideally, the bags should be tailored to fit the carrier and you must check that they fit securely in place. You should also make sure that they don't sway when you're descending at speed.

Frame-mounted extras

You can put almost anything on a bike frame, from a heart monitor to an electric motor.

Actually, heart monitors fit on the handlebars. If your main motive in cycling is fitness, they can help you assess just how hard you're working. It's easy to kid yourself that you're going flat out but once you know your own physiological capability, the heart monitor won't lie and will tell you just how well you're doing.

The sensor for the heart monitor fits under your shirt, but for bike computers, there is a magnetic sender on the front wheel, a pick-up taped to the forks and a read-out on the handlebars once again. The functions usually include time, elapsed time from the start of the journey and distance covered.

Luggage carriers and panniers have already been covered, but there are many ways of squeezing additional luggage on a bike. Some bags mount directly on the handlebars, but they're normally best with a front carrier to prevent contact with the front wheel. You can also attach anything from a small tool pack to a largish bag under the saddle, and, neatest of all, there are specially tailored bags that fit in the angle between top tube and seat tube. These, incidentally, double as padding when you carry your bike.

Brazed-on bosses are the key to fitting lots of smaller accessories like mini-pumps and emergency tool kits. The range is likely to expand in the next few years, so if you're buying a new bike, go for two sets of braze-ons, allowing one for accessories and the other for a water bottle.

As for the electric motor, it fits on the back wheel and you switch it on for going uphill. The trouble is it does away with all the pleasure of grinding up what often feels like a mountain side.

Bottle and Cage

1 Bottle cages are all designed to fit standard bottle bosses. Just undo the screw in the boss – they usually have an Allen head – position the cage and replace the screw.

Most pumps are carried on the frame, although a few riders keep them in a pack strapped under the saddle. Full-length pumps usually mount under the top tube: one end held by a small peg, the other nestling against the seat cluster. Mini-pumps can be mounted on clips supplied with the pump or on brazed-on bosses.

Chain stay protector

1 On the chain stay of any well-used bike, the paint slowly gets chipped away by the chain. The answer is a self-adhesive chain stay protector. First, check that the protector fits the curve of the chain stay and bend it to fit if necessary.

2 Next, degrease the chain stay with a solvent and remove the protective cover over the adhesive. Carefully place the protector down in position, then rub firmly with your thumb to improve adhesion.

2 This latest type of bottle cage is light, stylish and made of carbon fiber, so it's much stronger than it looks. Some riders prefer cages with rubber buttons for positive bottle retention.

TASTELESS

Aluminum water bottles are expensive, but they're far less likely to add a nasty taste to your drink than plastic ones. In winter, well-equipped riders use a thermos tailored to fit the standard bottle cage.

A lthough heavy and ugly, the frame-mounted U-lock is one of the best ways of stopping bike theft. The clip is plastic-covered, so it won't damage your frame and only requires two screws to hold it there. Some riders save a little weight by wrapping a chain and lock around the seat post.

S ome bikes come with a quick-release seat post binder, but they can be retro-fitted in materials from aluminum to titanium. Once you've got the hang of them, you can whip the saddle away in seconds, either to deter all but the toughest of thieves or to help fit your bike into a car or the luggage bay of a bus.

Children's seats and safety

Occasionally ideas from the car industry cross over into the world of bikes. The plastic child safety seat is one of the best so far.

Nearly all child seats are made from molded plastic. The designs are strongly influenced by the child seats used in cars and the net result is that it's now quite practical to think of carrying kids weighing up to about 40 pounds to the play group or the shops.

Different makers of child seats offer different features. The type shown in the steps here can be installed without interfering with an existing luggage carrier and, once the basic fittings are in place, it's a matter of seconds to attach the seat and remove it. This type also has foot rests that rule out any possibility of small feet getting caught in the wheel, plus cushioning and an effective shoulder harness. This type is also highly adjustable and fits more or less any bike.

Other types go on a luggage carrier using a simple slide-on mounting. Unfortunately, this rules out carrying any luggage at all at the back, but most riders probably find a child is enough of a handicap anyway. On the other hand, if there are several bikes in the family, the seat can be swapped between them simply by fitting them all with the correct type of carrier. The top-price child's seat has a movable bar that allows you to lift it off the carrier and use it as a picnic chair.

Never go off and leave a child in a safety seat unless someone is holding the bicycle steady.

1 Open up the clamp and slip it on to the down tube. To get the correct position, test-fit the seat and raise or lower clamp as necessary. Now tighten the mounting bolts but don't be surprised if you have to adjust the position later.

2 Test-fit the seat to check the height for the seat stay supports and when you've got it about right, tighten up the fittings. Then check that the seat fits easily on the ears and that the stay fits into the clamp without problems.

3 Adjust the position of the clamps and supports, if necessary, to ensure that the seat fits smoothly. Then position the front end of the stay in the frame clamp and press the red plastic locking tab down to hold it firmly in place.

4 The seat should still move about easily, allowing you to push the black plastic foot rests on to the round knobs on the seat stay. You then grasp the blue locking piece on each side, push them forward and turn them at the same time.

5 Turn the locking pieces through 90° to lock them. The seat should now be positioned well above the back wheel and the luggage carrier, and it should also feel firm and stable. The seat should be as close to the saddle as possible.

HELMET

SHOULDER HARNESS

PLASTIC-MOLDED SEAT BASE

FOOT RESTS WITH WHEEL GUARD

6 The carrier is now ready for the child to be lifted in. Be sure the feet are in the rests and adjust the harness. If you want to remove the seat, just lift the red locking tab and turn the blue locking pieces, then pull the seat back and off.

Bikes on cars

Roof and tow-bar mounting

The best way to enjoy the countryside is to take the bikes out of town by car, leaving the crowded cities far behind.

Roof racks are probably the best way of transporting bikes. On the positive side, there is enough room for up to four machines, they won't get covered in road dust or mud and you can get access to the luggage area without difficulty. On the other hand, they're not easy to load and create noise as well as aerodynamic drag. Rail-type bike carriers which hold a bike upright on both wheels can be fitted to nearly all roof racks. The bike is usually supported by an arm and this sometimes locks in place to improve theft resistance. The alternative way of mounting a bike to a roof rack uses a standard wheel quick-release fitted to the front of the roof rack. The forks are slotted in, without the front wheel, which reduces the aerodynamic drag and improves the steering in crosswinds.

Trunk-, tailgate- and tow-bar-mounted bike carriers create less noise and less aerodynamic drag, but when loaded, the back lights and license plate may be obscured. This is, of course, illegal. So check for visibility before buying one of these carriers. The only way around this is to wire the car for a light board and strap it on the stack of bikes every time.

Tow-bar-mounted racks are more secure than the strap-on type and come in two varieties. One type has a pair of horizontal arms and you simply throw the bikes on. The other type has tubular wheel supports and is still more secure. You can even obtain racks specially designed for off-road vehicles with the spare wheel mounted at the back.

1 This setup has a standard roof rack which is bolted on to the gutters and is fitted with rail carriers. If your car has permanent roof rails, you can usually add cross bars supplied by the main dealer or specialty accessory suppliers.

2 Each type of tow-bar-mounted bike carrier has a specific mounting plate that is bolted semi-permanently behind the tow ball. To carry a bike, you just fit the carrier into the mounting plate. With most carriers, you can tow a trailer at the same time.

PIPE INSULATION
Most roof racks and bike carriers are made of metal tubing and could seriously damage the paintwork on your car or bike if they're not well cushioned. When the original padding wears through, replace with the tubular insulation for water or heating pipes which comes in a couple of different sizes. If the plastic covering on the feet of a roof rack has worn through or torn, protect your paint by wrapping the bare metal in insulating tape. Don't cut the old covering off unless unavoidable.

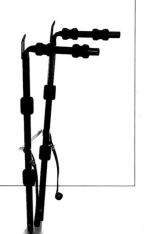

Strap-on bike carrier

1 Position the carrier so that the arms are at the top, stretch out the top straps and fit the clips over the lip of the tailgate or trunk lid. Then adjust the carrier up or down as necessary and level it off using the straps.

2 Next, the carrier is braced with the bottom strap. Find a suitable location, preferably the towing eyes, around the rear bumper or under the car to thread the strap through. Fit the end into the buckle on the carrier and pull tight.

3 Test the carrier to ensure that the straps are tight and that it's level. Check also that the protective rubber sleeving is OK. Then lift the bike on the carrier arms and settle it so that the wheels and pedals are well clear of the paintwork.

4 Strap the bike to the carrier and add some sort of lock so that the bike won't disappear at the next traffic lights. Finally, strap a light board to the bike and check that all the lights work correctly before you take to the road.

5 Two bikes, even three, can be carried on a strap-on rack but there is no doubt that such a load can never be completely stable. It's also obvious that the indicators and brake lights are hidden from other traffic, so budget for wiring up the light board. And don't forget about the bikes when you're backing up in a confined space or parking.

WHAT DOES THAT MEAN?

This section explains the meaning of words commonly used by bike enthusiasts, including American words that have entered biking 'language' since the advent of mountain bikes.

A

AHEADSET: *Japanese/American brand of headset. Can only be used with specially designed forks and stem. Tioga makes a similar setup.*

ALLEN KEY: *six-sided, L-shaped bar of metal that fits in to the socket of an Allen-head bolt. Available individually, in boxed sets, folding sets and on a ring.*

ALLOY: *usually short for aluminum alloy. A mixture of metals which is usually better than a pure one.*

ALLOY RIMS: *all decent quality bikes have wheel rims made of aluminum alloy. Steel is the alternative material but the braking surface is so smooth that it is hard to stop quickly, even with pads specially formulated for use with this material.*

ANTI-SEIZE COMPOUND: *a light grease containing powdered metal, usually copper. The grease evaporates, leaving the copper behind, which acts as a lubricant.*

AXLE: *the central part of a bearing assembly.*

B

BALL BEARING: *usually means a hard-chromed, perfectly round, steel ball that fits between the cup and cone in bike bearings. Also means the complete assembly of inner and outer race plus ball bearings, as used in a cartridge bottom bracket.*

BAR ENDS: *look like cow horns bolted to the ends of straight handlebars. They give an alternative hand position, especially useful for hill climbing or in traffic.*

BEADS: *the stiff edge of a tire. Usually made of wire but occasionally of Kevlar.*

BEARINGS: *any part designed to minimize the wear in a rotating or sliding assembly. On a bike the main bearings are the headset, bottom bracket and hub bearings.*

BINDER BOLT: *long bolt that fits in to the upright part of the stem and screws in to the cone or wedge that locks the stem in to the frame.*

BOTTLE BOSS: *threaded frame fitting used for attaching bottle cages to the frame.*

BOTTOM BRACKET: *the bearings and axle that carry the crankset.*

BOTTOM BRACKET SHELL: *the housing at the bottom of the seat and down tubes in to which the bottom bracket is fitted.*

BRAZED-ON FITTING: *items like bottle bosses and lever bosses attached permanently to the frame.*

BUTT: *the thickened end of a tube. See double butted.*

C

CABLE ENDCAP: *a soft metal sleeve that can be crimped on to the end of a cable to prevent it from fraying.*

CABLE STOP: *a hollow tube brazed on to the frame. The cable housing fits in to the open end, while the inner cable passes out of the other. Often slotted so that you can pull the housing out without disconnecting the inner cable — useful when lubricating the inner cable.*

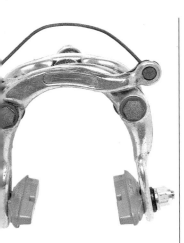

CANTILEVER BRAKES: *attached to the frame via pivots on the fork blades and chain stays. Powerful brakes, used on most mountain bikes because mud does not build up around them. Also used on hybrids and tourers.*

CARBON FIBER: *high-strength, high-cost material used for making frames, seat posts and other components. The fibers are usually woven in to a cloth or tape and bound together with resin. Very expensive and not suitable for everyday use.*

CARTRIDGE BOTTOM BRACKET: *bottom bracket bearing in which the axle runs on standard ball bearings, sealed inside a metal sleeve. Low maintenance. Becoming more and more popular.*

CENTERING: *usually refers to adjusting the position of a brake in such a way that the brake pads are equally spaced from the braking surface. Can also refer to fitting a back wheel so that it is equally spaced between the chain stays.*

CENTERPULL BRAKES: *a brake with two separate arms independently mounted on a back plate. Powerful and reliable but no longer made.*

CENTER TO CENTER: *usual way of measuring frame size. Distance from center of bottom bracket axle to center of top*

tube. The measurement can be given in either inches or centimeters – it makes no difference.*

CHAIN GUARD: *usually a light steel device that wraps around the chain, protecting the rider. Fixed to the frame with clips.*

CHAINRING: *the toothed part of the crankset which engages with the chain.*

CHAIN STAY: *the tube that runs between the bottom bracket and the dropout. It is usually oval near the bottom bracket.*

CHROME MOLYBDENUM OR CHROMOLY: *a steel alloy often used for bike frames. Though not a high-end material, chrome molybdenum steel is of good quality and ideal for budget-priced bikes.*

CLINCHERS: *detachable tires that are held on to the wheel rim by stiff beads that clinch under the open edges of the rim.*

CLUSTER: *usually short for sprocket cluster.*

COGS: *people often speak of the chainring and sprockets as cogs because they're toothed.*

COLUMBUS: *Italian maker of high-quality frame tubing.*

COTTERLESS CRANKS: *cranks that bolt on to the square end of the bottom bracket axle.*

COTTER PINS: *tapered steel pins with one flat side that hold the cranks on to the bottom bracket axle. Seldom found on recent bikes.*

CRANKS: *metal components that carry the pedals and transmit rider's energy to the chainring.*

CRANKSET: *the chainrings, spider and cranks are known collectively as the crankset.*

CUP AND CONE BEARING: *the standard bike bearing assembly consisting of ball bearings trapped between the semi-*

circular cup and the tapered cone. These bearings are adjusted by moving the screwed part in or out until they turn freely, without any play.*

D

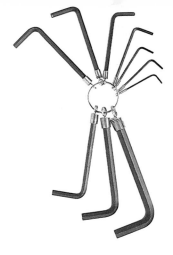

DEGREASER: *any solvent that will dissolve grease. Includes paraffin, diesel fuel and various specially formulated, ecologically acceptable brand-name products.*

DERAILLEUR: *French word for gearing sytems that work by 'derailling' the chain from one sprocket to another. Easily the most popular gearing system.*

DIAMOND FRAME: *the standard shape for a bike frame. Mountain bikes usually have a modified diamond frame.*

DOUBLE BUTTED: *used to describe frame tubing which is drawn thin in the middle for lightness and thicker at the ends where maximum strength is needed.*

DOWN TUBE: *usually the largest diameter part of the frame. Runs from the head tube to the bottom bracket.*

DRIVETRAIN: *all the components that deal with transmitting power from the rider's legs to the back wheel. That means crankset, chain and sprockets, plus the front and rear derailleurs.*

DROPOUT: *the part of the frame that carries the front or back wheel.*

DROPS: *short for drop handlebars found on road racing and touring bikes.*

DUAL PIVOT BRAKES: *a cross between sidepull and centerpull brakes. More compact than centerpulls and more powerful than sidepulls.*

F

FIXED GEAR: *a single sprocket screwed on to the rear hub, without a freewheel. All the time that the bike is moving, the rider has to pedal.*

FORK CROWN: *the top part of the forks. Sometimes it is separate, sometimes it is formed out of the fork blade itself.*

FORK END: *the part of the fork that carries the front wheel.*

FORKS: *the steerable part of the frame that holds the front wheel.*

FRAME ANGLES: *the angle between the top tube and seat tube; and between the top tube and head tube. Greatly influences how the frame behaves on the road.*

FREEHUB: *a recently introduced design of rear hub which has the sprocket cluster built in. Suitable for 7- or 8-speed setups, the right-hand hub bearing fits inside the cluster part.*

FREEWHEEL: *nearly all sprockets are mounted on a freewheel mechanism which allows you to coast along without pedalling.*

FRONT DERAILLEUR: *front gear mechanism that swaps the chain from one chainring to another. Two chainrings multiplies the number of gears by two. Three chainrings multiplies the number by three.*

G

GEAR HANGER: *the piece of metal that attaches the rear derailleur to the frame. Can be separate from, or part of, the frame.*

GEAR RANGE: *the gap between the lowest gear and the highest.*

GEAR RATIO: *on bikes, this is the number of inches that the bike will move for each revolution of the cranks. On a low gear, this is about 1 m (40 inches) per revolution and around 2.7 m (110 inches) on a high one.*

H

HAMMER: *a tool that should be used with caution on a bike.*

HEADSET: *the top and bottom bearings that support the forks and allow them to turn, thus providing steering. The bottom bearing is subject to very heavy loads and must be replaced when dents form in the bearing race.*

HEAD TUBE: *the shortest frame tube. Fits between the top and down tubes. Can be so short as to be almost non-existent on very small frames.*

HIGH GEAR: *a gear ratio in which you travel a long way for every revolution of the cranks. In high, the chain is on the largest chainring and one of the smallest sprockets.*

HUB GEARS: *the alternative system to derailleur gears. Contained within an enlarged rear hub. 3-, 5- and 7-speed versions now available but they all tend to be heavy and absorb a lot of energy.*

HYBRID: *type of bike combining some mountain bike components and frame features with large wheels and a fairly normal frame.*

I

INDEXED GEARS: *derailleur gears with a shifter that has click stops indicating each gear position.*

K

KEVLAR: *high-strength artificial fiber used for reinforcing tires and other components.*

KNOBBIES: *deeply treaded tires designed for high grip in dirt, rocks and mud.*

L

LOW GEAR: *a gear ratio in which you move a short distance for every revolution of the cranks. Used for climbing hills and off-road.*

LUBE: *short for lubricant.*

LUG: *a complex steel sleeve used to join the main tubes of a frame.*

N

NIPPLE: *the metal nut that passes through the rim and screws on to the spoke. Spokes are tensioned by tightening up the nipple.*

P

PHILLIPS SCREWDRIVER: *screwdriver with cross-shaped tip. Sizes 1 and 2 are both used on bikes and are not interchangeable.*

PLAY: *unwanted movement in a bearing. Can be due to wear or incorrect adjustment. Sometimes spoken of as 'a couple of milli-meters of play'.*

PRESTA VALVE: *found mainly on racing bike tyres. Has a knurled section on the end to keep it closed.*

PULLEY WHEELS: *small wheels that guide the chain around the sprockets and towards the chainring.*

Q

QUICK RELEASE: *usually refers to the mechanism that allows you to remove a bike wheel with just a turn of the quick release lever. Can also refer to other quick release components like seat post clamps and panniers.*

R

RACE: *part of a bearing assembly in contact with the ball bearings.*

REAR DERAILLEUR: *rear gear mechanism that deals with up to eight sprockets.*

REYNOLDS: *British makers of high-quality steel tubing for frames.*

RIM: *the part of the wheel on which the tire is mounted.*

ROADSTER: *old-fashioned sit-up-and-beg bike.*

S

SCHRADER VALVE: *the car-type tire valve that has a separate insert. Larger in diameter than a Presta valve.*

SEAT CLUSTER: *the area where the seat stays, down tube and top tube all come together.*

SEAT POST: *tube that fits in to the seat tube and supports the saddle.*

SEAT STAY: *the small-diameter tube that runs between the seat lug and the dropout.*

SEAT TUBE: *the large-diameter frame tube which supports the saddle.*

SHIFTER: *refers to any mechanism for changing gear.*

SIDEPULL BRAKE: *type of brake used on road bikes. Both brake arms are connected to the brake cable on one side of the unit.*

SLICKS: *smooth tires used on mountain bikes for road riding.*

SPOKE: *the thin wire component that connects the hub to the rim.*

SPRAY LUBE: *refers to various brands of silicone-based aerosol lubricant. Also to the specialist bike-type, which contains a solid lubricant that remains after the liquid part has evaporated.*

SPROCKET: *the toothed wheel or wheels attached to the back wheel that transfer drive from the chain to the hub.*

SPROCKET CLUSTER: *collective name for all the sprockets of a derailleur gear system.*

STEERER TUBE: *the tube that fits in to the fork crown and is supported by the headset. Turns with the fork.*

STEM: *fits in to the steerer tube and supports the handlebars.*

STI: *a gear-changing system made by Shimano in which the shifters are built in to the brake levers.*

STRADDLE CABLE: *short cable that joins two independent brake arms. Found on some cantilever and all centerpull brakes.*

SUSPENSION FORKS: *forks that allow the front wheel to move up and down to absorb bumps. The movement is usually controlled by some sort of spring and a gas or fluid damper mechanism.*

T

TIRE – 700C: *the type of tyre normally fitted to good-quality road bikes with 27-inch wheels. Thin, light and strong.*

TIRE VALVE: *device that holds air pressure in a tire. On a bike, the valve is actually part of the tube.*

TIRE WALL: *also referred to as the sidewall. The area of a tire between the tread and the wheel rim. Often a yellow color that contrasts with the black of the tread.*

TOE-IN: *usually measured in millimeters. Refers to fitting brake pads closer to the rim at the front than at the back.*

TOP TUBE: *the tube joining the seat tube to the head tube. It is usually horizontal but increasing numbers of bikes have a sloping top tube.*

TUBULARS: *a tire where the tube is sewn inside the tread part.*

W

WHEEL RIM: *the outer part of a bike wheel that carries the tire. Also the braking surface. Can be made of steel or alloy.*

WISHBONE STAY: *a design of chainstay in which the two tubes join above the back wheel and are connected to the seat cluster by a larger single tube.*

TROUBLESHOOTING

GENERAL

Riding discomfort
- *Adjust bar reach/position*
- *Adjust saddle fore/aft position and height*

Riding feels bumpy
- *Tires under inflated*
- *Install wider tires*

Saddle discomfort
- *Adjust saddle position/angle*
- *Try padded cycling shorts/tights*
- *Install better quality saddle*

Handlebar discomfort
- *Adjust handlebar angle*
- *Try different grips/padded bar tape*
- *Try cycling gloves*
- *Try a different bar shape*

Foot discomfort
- *Try shoes with firmer sole*
- *Check toe-clips are correct size*
- *Check foot position*

Bike tiring to ride
- *Tires under inflated*
- *Saddle too low*
- *Brakes rubbing wheel*
- *Tire rubbing frame or mudguard*
- *Transmission, chain corroded*
- *Inappropriate use of gears*
- *Fit narrower/slicker tires*

Bike unstable, especially at speed
- *Luggage too heavy, high, or far back*
- *Rack insufficiently rigid*
- *Tires under inflated*
- *Wheel/headset bearings loose*
- *Bent forks or frame*
- *Wheels need truing*

Bike rattles
- *Mudguards, rack, chainguard, or other accessories loose*

Scraping sounds
- *Mudguards rubbing on tire*
- *Mudflap or debris caught inside mudguard*
- *Chain rubbing chainguard*

Small bolts work loose
- *Reinstall with Loctite thread compound*

GEARS

REAR DERAILLEUR
Indexing imprecise/slow
- *Cable tension needs adjustment*
- *Cable needs greasing/replacing*
- *Derailleur or its hanger bent/misaligned*
- *Incompatible components*
- *Incorrect cable/cable housing/endcaps*

Can't get biggest cog
- *Rear derailleur's 'low' screw needs adjustment*
- *Cable tension needs adjustment*

Chain/derailleur goes into wheel
- *Rear derailleur's 'low' screw needs adjustment*
- *Derailleur or its hanger bent*
- *Check spokes and wheel ok*

Can't get smallest cog
- *Rear derailleur's 'high' screw needs adjustment*
- *Cable tension needs adjustment*

Chain leaves smallest rear cog
- *Rear derailleur's 'high' screw needs adjustment*

FRONT DERAILLEUR
Chain jams during shift
- *Front derailleur too low*
- *Chain too short*

Chain leaves/won't get small ring
- *Front derailleur's 'low' screw needs adjustment*

Chain leaves/won't get big ring
- *Front derailleur's 'high' screw needs adjustment*

Chain won't shift/slow to shift
- *Front derailleur too high*
- *Front derailleur's mounting angle incorrect*
- *Cage plates need slight bending inwards*

FRONT AND REAR DERAILLEUR
Gears self-change/go out of adjustment
- *Lever's tensioning bolt needs tightening*
- *Somebody oiled a friction lever!*
- *Cable anchor bolt loose*
- *Cable endcaps missing*

Shifting requires a lot of effort
- *Cable routing incorrect*
- *Cable needs lubrication/replacement*

HUB GEARS
Hub gear slips (all models)
- *Cable tension needs adjustment*
- *Cable clamps/guides loose*
- *Wheel slipping – nuts loose?*
- *Hub's internal parts worn*
- *Chain/sprocket severely worn*

CHAIN, PEDALS AND CRANKS

Chain broken
- *Chain joined incorrectly*
- *Chain worn*

Chain jumps under load
- *Chain and/or cassette cogs worn*
- *Stiff link*

Chain noisy
- *Chain needs lubrication*
- *Chain worn*

Regular clicking or jumping
- *Chain has stiff link*
- *Crank cotter pin loose/worn*
- *Crank bolt loose*
- *Bent cog/chainwheel tooth*

Irregular clicking/creaking when pedalling
- *Pedal cage or bearings disintegrating*
- *Bottom bracket bearings need attention*
- *Loose spokes*
- *Chainwheel bolts need greasing*
- *Crank loose on axle*
- *Last resort – grease axle taper*

Pedalling feels strange
- *Cranks or pedals bent or loose*

Back-pedalling feels stiff
- *Hub gear or single-speed chain too tight*
- *Hub gear bearings too tight*

Irregular knocking sound
- *Bottom bracket bearings need attention*

FREEWHEELS
Freewheel 'knocks' while pedalling
- *Its bearings are working loose!*

Freewheel spins noisily	◆ Its bearings are worn/need cleaning/lubrication
Freewheel slips/binds	◆ Mechanism needs attention/replacement
FREEHUBS Freehub slips/binds	◆ Shimano - replace freehub body ◆ Most others - overhaul it
Cassette 'knocks' in riding	◆ Cassette lockring loose

BRAKES

Insufficient brake power/cable pull	◆ Cable needs adjusting ◆ Quick-release needs resetting ◆ Brake pads worn ◆ Oil on rim ◆ Cable corroded or needs lubrication ◆ Brake lever mounting clamp loose ◆ Incompatible brake/lever combination
Brakes quickly lose power	◆ Cable anchor bolt insufficiently tight ◆ Brake pads not tight ◆ Cable housing missing endcaps
Brakes don't release properly	◆ Pivot bolt(s) too tight ◆ Cable corroded or needs lubrication ◆ Brake pad position incorrect ◆ Spring tension of brake incorrect
Brakes noisy/squeal	◆ Brake pads old and hard – replace ◆ Brake pads need 'toeing-in' ◆ Rim needs cleaning
Brakes chatter/grab	◆ Brake pads need 'toeing-in' ◆ Wheel rim bent or dented ◆ Brake pivots too loose ◆ Headset bearings loose
Brakes stiff to apply	◆ Cable corroded or not lubricated ◆ Cable routing too short or too long ◆ Spring tension of cantilever brakes set incorrectly
Brake levers creak in use	◆ Spray mounting and pivots with thin lubricant
Poor braking in rain	◆ Install better brake pads/alloy rims

WHEELS AND TIRES

Tire deflates slowly	◆ Slow puncture ◆ Valve loose or leaking
Tire deflates quickly	◆ Puncture or blowout!
Repetitive punctures	◆ Puncture cause still in tire ◆ Rim tape missing ◆ Protruding spoke ◆ Tire worn ◆ Tires under inflated ◆ Tire levers used to mount tire
Tire unevenly mounted	◆ Remount correctly
Wheel out of true	◆ Broken spoke ◆ Spokes need adjustment
Clicking noises from hub	◆ Bearings need attention
Wheels have side-to-side play	◆ Wheel bearings loose ◆ Wheel nuts loose ◆ Broken wheel spindle

BARS AND SADDLE

Bars don't appear or feel right	◆ Check alignment ◆ Check for bent bars
Bars creak	◆ Bar/stem interface needs greasing ◆ Stem/fork interface needs greasing ◆ Bars are developing a crack!
Bars rotate in stem	◆ Stem bolt insufficiently tight ◆ Incorrect matching of bars and stem
Handlebar stem moves in fork	◆ Stem binder bolt insufficiently tight
Handlebar stem seized in fork	◆ Stem wasn't greased. Try soaking with spray lubricant
Saddle tilts or moves	◆ Post's cradle bolt insufficiently tight ◆ Saddle clamp bolt insufficiently tight ◆ Saddle clamp too high on post
Saddle noisy or creaking	◆ Spray clamp, springs, etc. with light lubricant
Seat post seized in frame	◆ Post wasn't greased. Try soaking with spray lubricant ◆ Post diameter too large
Seat post moves in frame	◆ Seat post binder bolt insufficiently tight ◆ Post diameter too small

FRAME AND FORKS

Forks chatter	◆ Headset bearings loose ◆ Brakes grabbing rim
Bike tends to pull to one side	◆ Wheel (especially front) not centered ◆ Forks or frame bent
Steering/handling strange	◆ Tires under inflated ◆ Headset too tight/too loose ◆ Headset worn ◆ Forks/frame bent
Headset continually works loose	◆ Locknut insufficiently tight ◆ Worn headset ◆ Forks/frame bent ◆ Too many ball bearings!

BIKE EXTRAS

Battery lights don't work	◆ Batteries dead! – replace ◆ Batteries inserted wrong way around ◆ Bulbs blown – replace ◆ Electrical contacts need cleaning
Generator lights don't work	◆ Bulbs blown – replace ◆ Wiring faulty ◆ Bad contacts of lights and/or generator to frame ◆ Electrical contacts need cleaning ◆ Roller slipping
Generator noisy	◆ Roller incorrectly aligned ◆ Unsuitable tire wall ◆ Cheap generator
Computer doesn't register	◆ Sensor/magnet interface too great ◆ Sensor cable snagged or broken ◆ Computer not fully seated in bracket ◆ Computer/bracket contacts need cleaning

INDEX

AUTHOR'S ACKNOWLEDGMENTS
I would like to thank the following for all their help:

◆ Stuart at Lightweight Cycles, for sound advice and help (1, Ascot Parade, Clapham Park Road, London SW4. 0171 622 4818);
◆ Stratton Cycles, for loan of components and lots of information (101, East Hill, Wandsworth, London SW18. 0181 874 1381);
◆ Gordon Blair, for the loan of a bike;
◆ Sachs UK, for the loan of derailleurs;
◆ Fishers of Finchley, for the loan of Sachs off-road group set, hub gears and much help; and finally
◆ Michael Elson, for the loan of handlebars, stems and saddles (PO Box 5, Melton Mowbray, Leicestershire LE14 4SH).

PUBLISHER'S ACKNOWLEDGMENTS
The publisher would like to thank the following manufacturers and suppliers for kindly providing props for photography:

◆ Fishers of Finchley:bike accessories
◆ Halfords:Apollo and Carrera bikes, helmets, accessories, child seats and bicycle carrying racks
◆ Madison Cycles:Shimano components
◆ Krafft s.a.: lubricants and greases
◆ Trek UK: Trek bicycles, helmets, accessories and clothing
◆ Sachs UK: derailleurs

The publisher would also like to thank:
Margaret Barnard, Rose and Helena Beer, Jill Behr, Finny Fox-Davies, Tom Fox-Davies, Nick Fish, Nick Goodall, Hazlegrove School, Dave Hermelin, Dave Notley, Lucy Pope, Laura Potts, Ben Searle, and the Yeovil Cycle Centre.

Photographic credits
Key: t top, b bottom, l left, r right, m middle
Nick Pope: 36bl, bm, br; 37
Stockfile:4bl; br; 5; 17
Front Cover:Main picture by Image Bank (Kenneth Redding); other pictures by Tim Ridley, Steve Behr and Stockfile (Steve Behr, Bob Smith, Mark Gallup and Sue Darlow).